DIMENSIONAL
TUCK
KNITTING

DIMENSIONAL
TUCK
KNITTING

AN INNOVATIVE
TECHNIQUE
FOR CREATING
SURFACE DESIGN

Tracy Purtscher

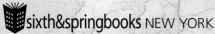
sixth&springbooks NEW YORK

sixth&springbooks

104 West 27 Street, Third Floor, New York, NY 10001
www.sixthandspring.com

Developmental Editor
JACOB SEIFERT

Art Director
JOE VIOR

Yarn Editor
JACLENE SINI

Supervising Patterns Editor
CARLA SCOTT

Patterns Editor
RENEE LORION

Technical Illustrator
LORETTA DACHMAN

Photography
JACK DEUTSCH

Copy Editor
SARAH PEASLEY

Vice President/Editorial
Director
TRISHA MALCOLM

Publisher
CAROLINE KILMER

Production Manager
DAVID JOINNIDES

President
ART JOINNIDES

Chairman
JAY STEIN

Library of Congress Cataloging-in-Publication Data

Names: Purtscher, Tracy, author.
Title: Dimensional tuck knitting : an innovative technique for creating
surface design / by Tracy Purtscher.
Description: First edition. | New York : Sixth&Spring Books,
[2017] | Includes index.
Identifiers: LCCN 2017002469 | ISBN 9781942021674 (hardcover)
Subjects: LCSH: Tuck knitting. | Knitting—Patterns.
Classification: LCC TT820 .P94 2017 | DDC 746.43/2—dc23
LC record available at https://lccn.loc.gov/2017002469

ISBN: 978-1-942021- 67-4

Manufactured in China

1 3 5 7 9 10 8 6 4 2

First Edition

Dedicated to the memory of my father
Wm. J. Grawey who made me who I am.
And to my husband Joe whose endless
love and understanding makes it possible
to be who I am.

CONTENTS

PROJECTS

WHAT IS DIMENSIONAL TUCK KNITTING?

When someone asks me what my book is about, my standard reply is, "It's a technique-based stitch dictionary for the hand knitter."

Non-knitters accept this as an answer to their question—no further explanation is needed nor wanted. Knitters, on the other hand, will want to know more. Hearing of a new stitch dictionary based on one particular technique always piques their interest and inspires a plethora of questions to which my answers are as follows:

. **No, there aren't any new stitches to learn. The most difficult skill needed is knitting or purling multiple stitches together.**

. **No, it isn't cabling, although a few stitches do look similar to cables.**

. **No, you don't need any tools other than your knitting needles and yarn.**

. **No, markers aren't required, although they can be helpful when using certain types of yarn.**

. **No, there isn't a lot of extra stitch or row counting.**

"Then what the heck is Dimensional Tuck Knitting?" asks the curious knitter.

"Well," I say, "It's a method of fabric manipulation developed for the hand knitter, based on a hand-sewing technique." The phrase "hand sewing" often throws them a bit, perhaps due to the fact that a large number of knitters see sewing only as a necessary evil during the finishing stages of their knits. Whenever I discuss my book with such a knitter and his or her eyes begin to glaze over at the mere mention of hand sewing, I quickly assure them there is no sewing required. This is often acknowledged with an audible sigh of relief. At this point in the conversation, most of the information I have offered is understood or, at the very least, accepted at face value. The next question is inevitably, "How did you come up with this?" I honestly don't know how to answer that question. You would probably have to walk around in my brain to understand how I connect the dots; but, frankly, most of the time I don't even understand how it happens. The best I can do is try to give you a brief synopsis of my synapses and describe the sequence of events that led me to this point.

People of a similar age to mine might remember a particular type of decorative pillow proudly displayed on their grandmothers' couches. These pillows were often made of cool, creamy satin or of voluptuous velvet with a nap so deep it danced beneath your fingertips. They came in a variety of sizes and shapes—squares, rectangles, bolsters, and the ubiquitous circles. Each pillow face was multifaceted with deep, deep folds and pleats creating complex allover designs or concentric labyrinths.

As a child, I was mesmerized by my grandmother's pillows. I remember reverently exploring the depths of the folds with timid fingers, trying to suss out the secret inner workings that created such beauty. I never could. To me, those pillows remained a magical mystery, a profound tactile memory emblazoned on my brain.

Fast forward more years than I care to admit to January 2013. Digging around in the sewing patterns of my favorite thrift store, I found a vintage McCall's pattern—Pattern #2467, to be precise. It was a pattern for three pleated pillows, not exactly like my grandmother's, but of the same technique. My heart leapt, and I knew in an instant I wanted to savor every moment of this discovery. It had to be done right, with all the pomp and circumstance called

for by the occasion, which meant waiting until I was home to unveil the secrets the pattern envelope contained. The long drive home, made even longer by anticipation, nearly killed me. It was one of the very few times I have actually cursed the far-flung seclusion of my home.

Once home, I settled quickly into my favorite thinking/wishing/what-if chair. I slowly opened the envelope flap with a deep breath and more than a little trepidation. The promise of the knowledge a childhood me could not even fathom was just too good to be true. My heart raced. The yellowed, brittle pages resisted my initial gentle tug but then let go and fluttered to my lap. What would they reveal? What would I learn?

Not much, as it turned out. I was underwhelmed. Oh heck, let's be frank: I was downright devastatingly disappointed. One childhood mystery blown to smithereens by a couple of sheaves of crumbling paper. McCall's Pattern #2467 contained nothing more than a single page of instruction and a very large dot-grid. It was all so simple, requiring none of the needle magic or advanced skills I had imagined—simply transfer the dot-grid to your fabric and connect the dots with a few whip stitches. I felt duped.

Even knowing my expectations had been set impossibly high—had been inflated by a childhood memory of some sort of needle magic—I had still gotten caught up in the moment of discovery. Just because I had imagined a secret of grand importance was hidden within didn't mean it actually was. After all, it was only a vintage home décor sewing pattern for pleated pillows. Heavy-hearted, I banished the pattern and all its too-simple bogus trickery to my nice-novelty-technique-to-try-sometime list. A list very seldom visited, and where ideas go to die. A fitting and just punishment for non-existent needle magic and innocence lost.

The remainder of 2013 was a blur. I was chosen to be a contestant in *The Fiber Factor*, Skacel's design competition,

similar to *Project Runway*, but for knitwear. Challenge 4, the knitting-machine challenge, provided an excellent opportunity for me to explore knitted welts as a means of shaping a garment. I had dabbled before with welts, turned hems, and pleats, but I remembered all too well the error-filled frustrations I had faced trying to count rows or stitches. Given those memories, I opted to hand sew all of my welts.

As I laboriously hand sewed a *lot* of welts on the wrong side of miles of stockinette, I noticed how all those little purl bumps lined up in straight rows and columns—a lot like graph paper. I thought, "Dang, if I sprinkled a few knit stitches amid the purl bumps, each oddball knit stitch could mark the proper rows to make the welts. And *that* would eliminate all this extra counting and double checking!" I followed my thoughts further, seeing in my mind's eye an ever-expanding grid of single oddball knit stitches scattered across a field of purls. But then, instead of graph paper, it looked like a dot-graph. And that's when it hit me: the proverbial light bulb moment.

However briefly I had scanned the contents of McCall's Pattern #2467 six months prior, I had understood the concept. I knew I could knit a dot-grid pattern. I knew, instead of whip stitching the dots together, I could knit or purl them together. And I knew then that I could knit the stitches from Grandmother's pillows! I made two very small swatches using a couple of the pillow patterns as my guide, incorporating tweaks appropriate for hand knitting. The concept of Dimensional Tuck Knitting was born. All the deep, deep dimensional folds, pleats, and tucks of Grandmother's pillows, created organically with sticks and string for the hand knitter—no sewing required.

NATURE & MECHANICS
OF DIMENSIONAL TUCKS

Dimensional Tuck Knitting is a method of fabric manipulation that relies on three primary factors: the strategic placement of Dimensional Tucks, the push-me/pull-you effect of divergent row gauges between adjacent stitch patterns, and the scale of the Dimensional Tuck stitch pattern. Let's examine these factors a bit more in depth to better understand each of their effects.

FACTOR 1: The Dimensional Tuck

Dimensional Tuck Knitting furthers the technique of knitted welts. By strategically placing simple tucks of only one or two stitches, you can make your fabric fold and bubble in unique and beautiful new ways. Tucks can be made from a stitch several rows directly below the live stitches, or from a stitch several rows below *and* a number of stitches to the left or right. If worked from directly below, a horizontal welt will appear, much like a traditional welt. If worked from below *and* to either side, the welt will appear as a diagonal. Inserting multiple tucks into your fabric allows them to combine into exciting new textures.

FACTOR 2: The Background Stitch

The background stitch is the pattern that appears directly on either side of your Dimensional Tuck stitch pattern. It will enhance the look and definition of your Dimensional Tuck stitch pattern and serve an integral role in the behavior and depth of texture in the resulting fabric.

To demonstrate the effect a background stitch has on a Dimensional Tuck stitch pattern, I have knit a few example swatches (see photos 1, 2, & 3). Each pairing features the same Dimensional Tuck stitch pattern on a garter background (left) and on a stockinette background (right).

Notice the lessening of depth and definition of the patterns worked on stockinette backgrounds. What comes into play here is the row gauge of the pattern stitch versus the row gauge of the background stitch. Garter stitch has a much tighter row gauge than stockinette. When knit as a background, garter stitch scrunches up the pattern stitch, adding depth and definition to the fabric. While I have knit all of the swatches in this book with garter backgrounds for maximum definition, a looser background stitch can be used if a subtler texture is desired.

It is possible to minimize the watering down of depth and definition while still using a stockinette or reverse stockinette background—simply insert a single

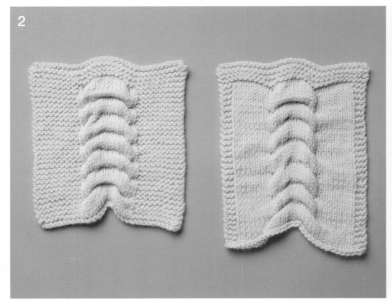

stitch as a divider between the pattern stitch and the background stitch. Given here are three samples of #49 Basic Upward Braid (see page 79) demonstrating this effect.

To the right, photo 4 has a garter background, photo 5 has a stockinette background, and photo 6 has a reverse stockinette background. Photos 5 & 6 have one extra stitch added before and after the pattern stitches. Think of these stitches as dividers between the pattern stitches and the background stitches. They stand alone unto themselves and are consistently knit on the wrong-side rows and slipped with the yarn in back on the right-side rows. This small but important addition returns *some* of the depth and definition lost when working with stockinette and reverse stockinette backgrounds.

The following page offers four additional background stitches you might want to use instead of garter stitch. These stitches have been chosen specifically for their similarity in row gauge to garter stitch, yet a word of caution is needed: These stitches do not create the same squishy, pliable fabric we associate with garter stitch. They work best in small doses, used between stitch repeats or between different stitch patterns.

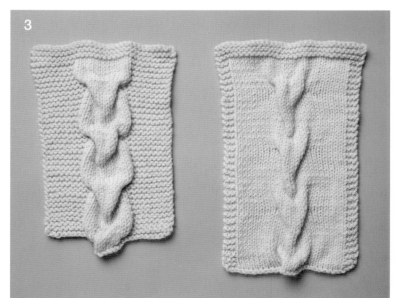

Pebble Stitch

RS *P1, sl 1 wyib; rep from * to last st, p1.
WS Knit

Reverse Pebble Stitch

RS Knit.
WS *P1, sl 1 wyib; rep from * to last st, p1.

Woven Purl Stitch

RS Purl.
WS *Sl 1 wyif, sl 1 wyib; rep from * to end.

Reverse Woven Purl Stitch

RS *Sl 1 wyib, sl 1 wyif; rep from * to end.
WS Knit.

FACTOR 3: Scale

The final factor that can alter the look and behavior of a Dimensional Tuck stitch pattern is scale, determined by the number of stitches and rows worked between the Tuck Stitch (a strategically placed knit or purl stitch, indicated by the colored boxes in the chart below) and the Pairing Stitch (a live stitch on the needle, indicated by the triangles in the chart below). While most swatches in this book are worked at a scale of 3x3 (3 stitches and 3 rows) or 3x5 (3 stitches and 5 rows), a Dimensional Tuck's scale may need to be changed for a number of reasons.

Aesthetics

Dimensional Tucks can look crisp, deep, and well-defined, but they can also be softened by increasing the scale of the pattern. Below are three examples of #45 Simple Left Twist and #46 Simple Right Twist (see page 75) worked in three different scales. Notice how the swatch on the left in a 3x3 scale looks firmer and more robust, whereas the twists of the center swatch are more fluid in a 3x5 scale. The swatch at the right in a 3x7 scale appears even softer and more fluid.

Structure

Structural soundness should be considered when contemplating changes in scale. Yarns known for having good stitch definition adapt to changes in scale very well, but other types may have special considerations that need to be addressed. For example, a fine yarn like mohair, typically worked in a loose gauge, might not have enough volume or substance to create deep folds. Increasing the scale in both the number of stitches and the number of rows could solve this problem by creating more fabric within the stitch pattern. How many stitches and how many rows is limited to how well each individual Tuck Stitch can maintain its shape without stretching out due to the weight of the added fabric. A super-bulky yarn may also require a change in scale. Because of the girth of the yarn itself, an increase in scale is usually needed to give the tuck enough room to comfortably fold back onto itself without distorting the stitches.

Convenience

Another reason one might have for changing the scale of a Dimensional Tuck has little to do with aesthetics or structure and is merely for the sake of convenience. Changing the scale by one stitch in width or by a couple of rows in height will have minimal effect on appearance or structure, but could greatly enhance ease of knitting when inserting a Dimensional Tuck stitch pattern into another project pattern.

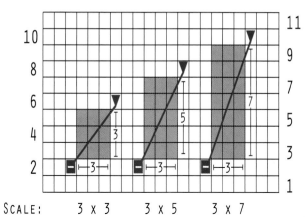

SCALE: 3 X 3   3 X 5   3 X 7
(STITCHES X ROWS)

CREATING A TUCK STITCH

Aside from being able to knit and purl, the most important skill knitters must have to successfully employ the Dimensional Tuck Knitting method is the ability to read their knitting.

In a perfect world, all knitters would be able to look at their knitting and know exactly what is happening and what to do next; but sometimes it's just not that easy, and sometimes you just don't want to think too much. Dimensional Tuck Knitting was developed with this in mind.

Even the most novice among us can look at a section of stockinette and spot the lone stitch that doesn't look like it belongs. Errors in our knitting usually jump out at us. I've exploited this knitterly trait and have used it as a key element in this technique. Every Dimensional Tuck is worked over a tidy base of stockinette stitch, but you will purposefully create oddball stitches that will jump out at you.

The first step in working any Dimensional Tuck is creating a Tuck Stitch. To do so, you will strategically place a lone knit stitch within a field of purl stitches, or a lone purl stitch within a field of knit stitches. In the charts throughout this book, this stitch is called a Tuck Stitch.

A strange and wonderful cause-and-effect happens when you do this—it creates an eye-catching anomaly in the fabric. Look at photo 1. Notice the break in the continuity of purl bumps. Note how the eye-catching purl bump highlights the legs of the stitch above it. This anomaly *caused* by the lone knit stitch in a field of purl stitches indicates where you will place your needle to complete a Dimensional Tuck. It is the legs of this anomaly that I ultimately think of as the Tuck Stitch.

When it comes time to complete a Dimensional Tuck, you will enlist your knitterly eye, spot the anomaly, pick up the legs of the Tuck Stitch (see photo 2), and work them together with one or more specific live stitches on your needles, also known as Pairing Stitches. I will later explain exactly how you work the Tuck Stitch together with the Pairing Stitch, but at this point all I want is for you to be able to see the legs of the Tuck Stitch that will be used to complete a Dimensional Tuck.

One of the most exciting things inherent in this oddball-stitch-as-a-marker philosophy is that it eliminates a good amount of counting. You will still have a healthy dose of the typical mantra-like counting we knitters use while in the knitting zone (k2, p2, k2, p2, k2, p2 . . . sound familiar?), but using Tuck Stitches eliminates the need to stop the flow of rhythmic knitting to count X stitches to the right or left and then Y rows down.

NOTE TO KNITTING SCHOLARS

Yes. You're right. The Tuck Stitches indicated on the charts are not the stitches you pick up to complete your Dimensional Tucks. They are actually two different stitches in two different rows. To the casual eye, they seem like the same stitch; so I have blurred the line between them and refer to them as a single entity for purposes of this technique. It's better to simply enjoy the magic and not get bogged down in the how and why of this bewitching stitch-craft.

1

2

METHODS: STANDARD VS ALTERNATIVE

A large percentage of the patterns and projects in this book are worked using a standard method, but a few Dimensional Tuck stitch patterns using alternative methods have been sprinkled throughout the book to pique the interest of the adventurous. Detailed instructions for every stitch in this book appear in the next section, but a thorough understanding of the core differences between each method is advisable.

Regardless of method used, the core concept of a Dimensional Tuck remains the same. You always work over stockinette stitch, create Tuck Stitches, pick up Tuck Stitches, and work Tuck Stitches together with Pairing Stitches.

The differences between the methods are determined by three simple factors: the side of the fabric that is facing, how you pick up the Tuck Stitches, and how the Tuck Stitches are worked together with the Pairing Stitches.

Note If the correct method to use is not indicated in the written instructions, it will appear in the stitch key of the accompanying chart.

STANDARD METHOD
On WS
With the *wrong side* of the fabric facing, the Tuck Stitch is picked up *on the wrong side*. The Tuck Stitch is then worked by *purling* it together with the Pairing Stitch.

ALTERNATIVE METHODS
From RS
With the *wrong side* of the fabric facing, reach with your needle behind the work to the right side and pick up the Tuck Stitch *from the right side*. The Tuck Stitch is then worked by *purling* it together with the Pairing Stitch.

EXAMPLE Front panel of Front & Center Sweater (see pages 154–158). Note that the standard ON WS method and alternative FROM RS method are both used.

On RS
Note In this method, the Tuck Stitch presents itself as the legs *under* a prominent purl bump (see photos below), the legs of the purl bump itself.

With the *right side* of the fabric facing, the Tuck Stitch is picked up *on the right side*. The Tuck Stitch is then worked by *knitting* it together with the Pairing Stitch *through the back loops*.

EXAMPLE Compare swatches #22 Flame and #23 Smoke (see pages 52–53). These use the same Dimensional Tuck, but #22 Flame is worked in the alternative ON RS method while #23 Smoke is worked in the standard ON WS method, creating entirely different results.

From WS
Note This method is typically used when working Dimensional Tucks in the round.

With the *right side* of the fabric facing, reach with your needle behind the work to the wrong side and pick up the Tuck Stitch *from the wrong side*. The Tuck Stitch is then *knitted* together with the Pairing Stitch *through the back loops*.

EXAMPLES Luxury Fingerless Mitts (see pages 138–141), Dreamweaver Cowl (see pages 142–145), and Lucky Hat (see pages 150–153).

1

2

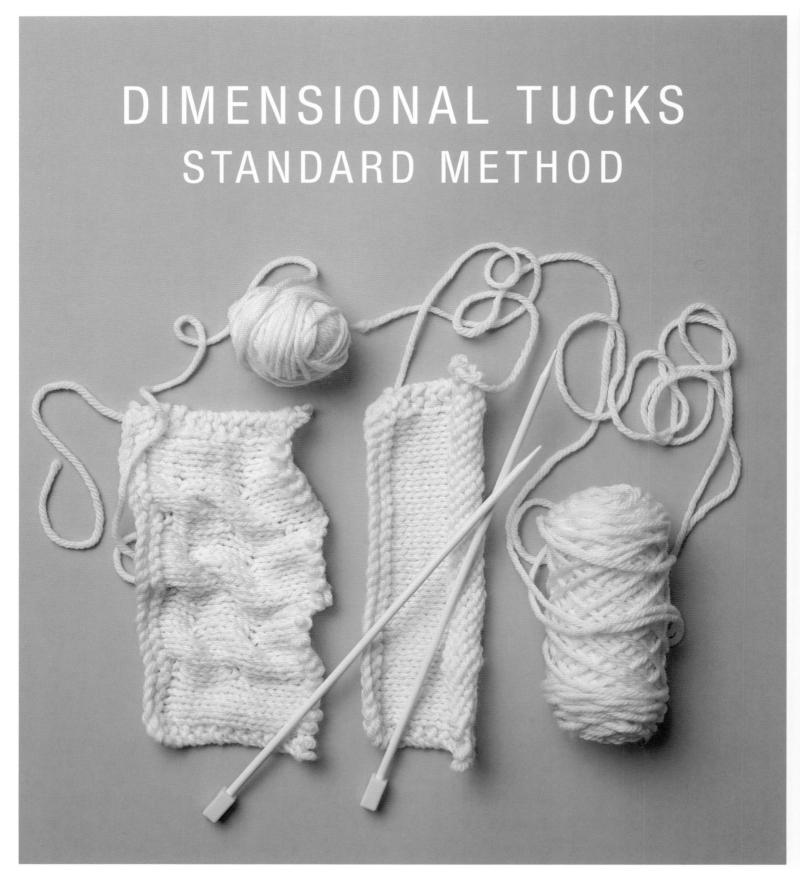

DIMENSIONAL TUCKS
STANDARD METHOD

LTT on WS
(LEFT TUCK TOGETHER ON WS)

1) With WS facing and yarn in front, slip Pairing Stitch to RH needle.

2) With RH needle, pick up both legs of Tuck Stitch located below LH needle and place them on LH needle.

3) Slip Pairing Stitch to LH needle. Purl Pairing Stitch and both legs of Tuck Stitch together.

RTT on WS
(RIGHT TUCK TOGETHER ON WS)

1) With WS facing, use LH needle to pick up both legs of Tuck Stitch below RH needle.

2) Slide legs of Tuck Stitch closer to Pairing Stitch.

3) Purl both legs of Tuck Stitch and Pairing Stitch together.

DRTT on WS (DOWN RIGHT TUCK TOGETHER ON WS)

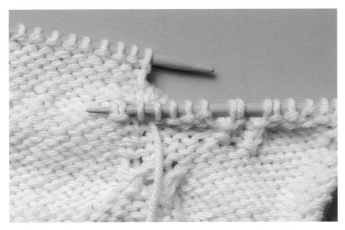

1) With WS facing, use RH needle to pick up both legs of Tuck Stitch below Pairing Stitch on LH needle and place them on LH needle.

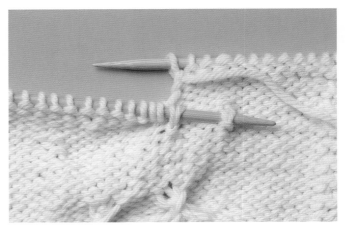

2) With LH needle, pick up both legs of Tuck Stitch below RH needle. Purl all legs of both Tuck Stitches together. Slip stitch just made to LH needle and purl it together with Pairing Stitch.

LDTT on WS (LEFT DOWN TUCK TOGETHER ON WS)

1) With WS facing and yarn in front, slip Pairing Stitch to RH needle. With RH needle, pick up both legs of Tuck Stitch below LH needle and place them on LH needle.

3) Purl all legs of both Tuck Stitches together. Slip stitch just made and Pairing Stitch to LH needle.

2) With LH needle, pick up both legs of Tuck Stitch below Pairing Stitch.

4) Purl two slipped stitches together.

DTT on WS (DOWN TUCK TOGETHER ON WS)

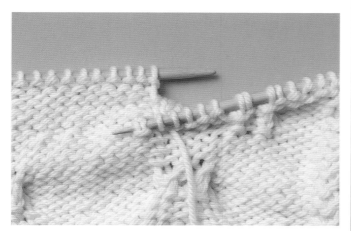

1) With WS facing, use RH needle to pick up both legs of Tuck Stitch directly below Pairing Stitch.

2) Place both legs of Tuck Stitch on LH needle.

3) Purl both legs of Tuck Stitch and Pairing Stitch together.

LRTT on WS (LEFT RIGHT TUCK TOGETHER ON WS)

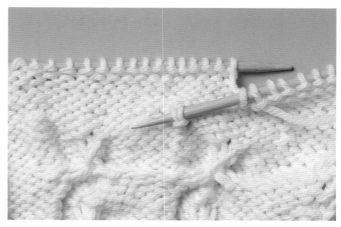

1) With WS facing and yarn in front, slip Pairing Stitch to RH needle. With RH needle, pick up both legs of Tuck Stitch below LH needle and place them on LH needle.

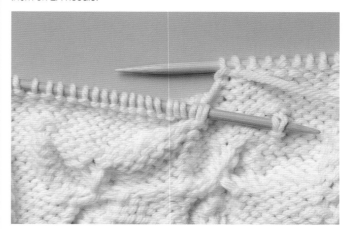

2) With LH needle, pick up both legs of Tuck Stitch below RH needle.

3) Purl all legs of both Tuck Stitches together. Slip stitch just made and Pairing Stitch to LH needle and purl them together.

SL#RTT on WS (SHARED LEFT RIGHT TUCK TOGETHER ON WS)

1) With WS facing and yarn in front, slip Pairing Stitch to RH needle. With RH needle, pick up *right leg only* of Tuck Stitch below LH needle. Slip picked-up leg and Pairing Stitch to LH needle and purl them together.

2) Work designated number of stitches (indicated by number in stitch abbreviation or stitches between Pairing Stitches on chart). With LH needle, pick up remaining *left leg* of same Tuck Stitch.

3) Purl second Pairing Stitch and *left leg* of Tuck Stitch together.

DRTT on WS (Down Right Tuck Together on WS)
Note Two Tuck Stitches are worked together with one Pairing Stitch. With WS facing and yarn in front, use RH needle to pick up both legs of Tuck Stitch directly below Pairing Stitch (first stitch on LH needle) and place them on LH needle. With LH needle, pick up both legs of Tuck Stitch below RH needle. Purl all legs of both Tuck Stitches together. Slip stitch just made to LH needle and purl it and Pairing Stitch together.

DRTT from WS (Down Right Tuck Together from WS)
Note Two Tuck Stitches are worked together with one Pairing Stitch. With RS facing and yarn in back, use RH needle to reach behind work to WS to pick up both legs of Tuck Stitch directly below Pairing Stitch (first stitch on LH needle) and place them on LH needle. With LH needle, reach behind work to WS to pick up both legs of Tuck Stitch below RH needle. Knit all legs of Tuck Stitches together through back loops. Slip stitch just made to LH needle and knit it and Pairing Stitch together through back loops.

DTT on WS (Down Tuck Together on WS)
With WS facing and yarn in front, use RH needle to pick up both legs of Tuck Stitch directly below Pairing Stitch (first stitch on LH needle) and place them on LH needle. Purl both legs of Tuck Stitch and Pairing Stitch together.

DTT from WS (Down Tuck Together from WS)
With RS facing and yarn in back, use RH needle to reach behind work to WS to pick up both legs of Tuck Stitch directly below Pairing Stitch (first stitch on LH needle) and place them on LH needle. Knit Tuck Stitch and Pairing Stitch together through back loops.

LDTT on WS (Left Down Tuck Together on WS)
Note Two Tuck Stitches are worked together with one Pairing Stitch. With WS facing and yarn in front, slip Pairing Stitch (first stitch on LH needle) to RH needle. With RH needle, pick up both legs of Tuck Stitch below LH needle and place them on LH needle. With LH needle, pick up both legs of Tuck Stitch directly below slipped Pairing Stitch. Purl all legs of both Tuck Stitches together. Slip stitch just made and slipped Pairing Stitch to LH needle and purl them together.

TUCK STITCH
An oddball stitch used to create an anomaly in the fabric, and the stitch legs accentuated by that anomaly.

PAIRING STITCH
A live stitch on the needle indicating the place where one or more Tuck Stitches are to be picked up to complete a Dimensional Tuck.

TUCK INSTRUCTIONS & TERMS

LDTT from WS (Left Down Tuck Together from WS)
Note Two Tuck Stitches are worked together with one Pairing Stitch.
With RS facing and yarn in back, slip Pairing Stitch (first stitch on LH needle) to RH needle. With RH needle, reach behind work to WS to pick up both legs of Tuck Stitch below LH needle and place them on LH needle. With LH needle, reach behind work to WS to pick up both legs of Tuck Stitch directly below slipped Pairing Stitch. Knit all legs of both Tuck Stitches together through back loops. Slip stitch just made and slipped Pairing Stitch to LH needle and knit them together through back loops.

LRTT on WS (Left Right Tuck Together on WS)
Note Two Tuck Stitches are worked together with one Pairing Stitch.
With WS facing and yarn in front, slip Pairing Stitch (first stitch on LH needle) to RH needle. With RH needle, pick up both legs of Tuck Stitch below LH needle and place them on LH needle. With LH needle, pick up both legs of Tuck Stitch below RH needle. Purl all legs of both Tuck Stitches together. Slip stitch just made and slipped Pairing Stitch to LH needle and purl them together.

LRTT from WS (Left Right Tuck Together from WS)
Note Two Tuck Stitches are worked together with one Pairing Stitch.
With RS facing and yarn in back, slip Pairing Stitch (first stitch on LH needle) to RH needle. With RH needle, reach behind work to WS to pick up both legs of Tuck Stitch below LH needle and place them on LH needle. With LH needle, reach behind work to WS to pick up both legs of Tuck Stitch below RH needle. Knit all legs of both Tuck Stitches together through back loops. Slip stitch just made and slipped Pairing Stitch to LH needle and knit them together through back loops.

LRTT on RS (Left Right Tuck Together on RS)
Note Two Tuck Stitches are worked together with one Pairing Stitch.
With RS facing and yarn in back, slip Pairing Stitch (first stitch on LH needle) to RH needle. With RH needle, pick up both legs of Tuck Stitch below LH needle and place them on LH needle. With LH needle, pick up both legs of Tuck Stitch below RH needle. Knit all legs of both Tuck Stitches together through back loops. Return stitch just made and slipped Pairing Stitch to LH needle and knit them together through back loops.

LRTT from RS (Left Right Tuck Together from RS)
Note Two Tuck Stitches are worked together with one Pairing Stitch.
With WS facing and yarn in front, slip Pairing Stitch (first stitch on LH needle) to RH needle. With RH needle, reach behind work to RS to pick up both legs of Tuck Stitch below LH needle and place them on LH needle. With LH needle, reach behind work to RS to pick up both legs of Tuck Stitch below RH needle. Purl all legs of both Tuck Stitches together. Slip stitch just made and slipped Pairing Stitch to LH needle and purl them together.

LTT on WS (Left Tuck Together on WS)
With WS facing and yarn in front, slip Pairing Stitch (first stitch on LH needle) to RH needle. With RH needle, pick up both legs of Tuck Stitch below LH needle and place them on LH needle. Return slipped Pairing Stitch to LH needle and purl it and both legs of Tuck Stitch together.

LTT from WS (Left Tuck Together from WS)
With RS facing and yarn in back, slip Pairing Stitch (first stitch on LH needle) to RH needle. With RH needle, reach behind work to WS to pick up both legs of Tuck Stitch below LH needle and place them on LH needle. Return slipped Pairing Stitch to LH needle and knit Pairing Stitch and legs of Tuck Stitch together through back loops.

RTT on WS (Right Tuck Together on WS)
With WS facing and yarn in front, use LH needle to pick up both legs of Tuck Stitch below RH needle. Purl legs of Tuck Stitch and Pairing Stitch (first stitch following legs of Tuck Stitch) together.

RTT from WS (Right Tuck Together from WS)
With RS facing and yarn in back, use LH needle to reach behind work to WS to pick up both legs of Tuck Stitch below RH needle. Knit legs of Tuck Stitch and Pairing Stitch (next stitch on LH needle) together through back loops.

SL#RTT on WS (Shared Left Right Tuck Together on WS)
Note One Tuck Stitch is worked together with two Pairing Stitches; each leg of Tuck Stitch is worked with a different Pairing Stitch.
With WS facing and yarn in front, slip Pairing Stitch (first stitch on LH needle) to RH needle. With RH needle, pick up *right leg only* of Tuck Stitch below LH needle and place it on LH needle. (**Note** You can place a marker into *left leg* of Tuck Stitch to make it easier to find later.) Return slipped Pairing Stitch to LH needle and purl it and *right leg* of Tuck Stitch together. Work designated number of stitches (number replacing # in stitch abbreviation). With LH needle, pick up remaining *left leg* of same Tuck Stitch, now below RH needle. Purl *left leg* of Tuck Stitch and Pairing Stitch (next stitch on LH needle) together.

SL#RTT from WS (Shared Left Right Tuck Together from WS)
Note One Tuck Stitch is worked together with two Pairing Stitches; each leg of Tuck Stitch is worked with a different Pairing Stitch.
With RS facing and yarn in back, slip Pairing Stitch (first stitch on LH needle) to RH needle. With RH needle, reach behind work to WS to pick up *right leg only* of Tuck Stitch below LH needle and place it on LH needle. (**Note** You can place a marker into *left leg* of Tuck Stitch to make it easier to find later.) Return slipped Pairing Stitch to LH needle and knit it and *right leg* of Tuck Stitch together through back loops. Work designated number of stitches (number replacing # in stitch abbreviation). With LH needle, reach behind work to WS to pick up remaining *left leg* of same Tuck Stitch, now below RH needle. Knit *left leg* of Tuck Stitch and Pairing Stitch (next stitch on LH needle) together through back loops.

DIMENSIONAL TUCK STITCHES

 LTT on WS
RTT from WS

 RTT on WS
LTT from WS

 DTT on WS
DTT from WS

 LDTT on WS
DRTT from WS

 DRTT on WS
LDTT from WS

 LRTT on WS
LRTT from WS
LRTT on RS
LRTT from RS

 SL#RTT on WS
SL#RTT from WS

READING THE CHARTS

Charts for Dimensional Tuck Knitting are not much different from other knitting charts. A grid is used to indicate each stitch with specific symbols, rows are numbered along the sides, and pattern repeats are clearly outlined. The only things that may throw you for a loop are the symbols that represent the Dimensional Tuck stitches themselves, but there is no need to worry. As soon as you learn how to read the symbols they will make perfect sense. The first thing to understand is that the symbol for each of the various stitches has three parts: the Tuck Stitch, the Pairing Stitch, and the Gathering Line.

The Tuck Stitch (A) appears as a colored box at the bottom of the stitch. This will coincide with the typical "P on RS, K on WS" symbol you've seen countless times before, and you will work it accordingly. This is the stitch that will cause the anomaly that will highlight the legs of the Tuck Stitch.

The Pairing Stitch (B) appears as an upside-down triangle or a circle. Once you reach this stitch, you will lift the leg(s) of the Tuck Stitch(es) onto the needle to complete a Dimensional Tuck.

The Gathering Line (C) appears as a colored line that connects a Pairing Stitch to one or two Tuck Stitches. As there may be multiple Tuck Stitches in your fabric at any given time, things may become a bit confusing. If you ever find yourself scratching your head trying to find the correct Tuck Stitch, simply consult your chart for a quick visual. The following page describes how Gathering Lines can help you visualize what your fabric will look like once the tucks are complete.

You will notice that the symbols for the Dimensional Tucks appear in different colors throughout this book. Unless otherwise noted within the pattern, these colors are not important and were chosen solely to match the color scheme of each section.

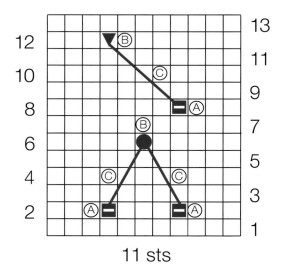

11 sts

22

SEEING THE PATTERN IN THE CHART

Whether they are for lace, cables, or colorwork, most charts provide a good visual of what the actual pattern will look like before the first stitch is even made. Dimensional Tuck Knitting charts often provide a good idea of what the fabric will look like, but if you don't know how to properly "read" them you will probably visualize a mirrored image of the pattern. No need to worry. I have come up with a trick for you to "see" the patterns from the charts.

To "read" your charts, you need to understand how the fabric will be manipulated as the Tuck Stitch is brought up to its corresponding Pairing Stitch on the needle. A Dimensional Tuck that is lifted directly upward (such as the DTT) will appear as a horizontal bulge in your fabric. A Dimensional Tuck that is lifted diagonally (such as the LTT or RTT) will appear as a diagonal bulge leaning in the opposite direction of its Gathering Line on the chart. The physical Dimensional Tuck will always cross its Gathering Line to create a plus sign for vertical Dimensional Tucks (DTT) or an X for diagonal Dimensional Tucks (LTT, RTT, etc.).

While it is easy to grasp this concept, visualizing multiple tucks at once can be tricky. Another helpful trick is to shade in your chart, creating the appropriate Xs and plus signs. Below is the chart for swatch #73 Half Hitch (see page 105). Notice the shadings and how they intersect the Gathering Lines. Now compare the shaded chart to the image of the actual knitted sample with the symbol for each Dimensional Tuck placed over it.

This method of "reading" the chart will work for any Dimensional Tuck pattern, but please keep in mind that this will only give a general idea of the fabric's final texture. Your fabric will bend and fold in small and unexpected ways where the tucks crash into each other, creating extra character and detail. You should also keep in mind that one swatch may look slightly different from another depending on tension, yarn, scale, and so forth.

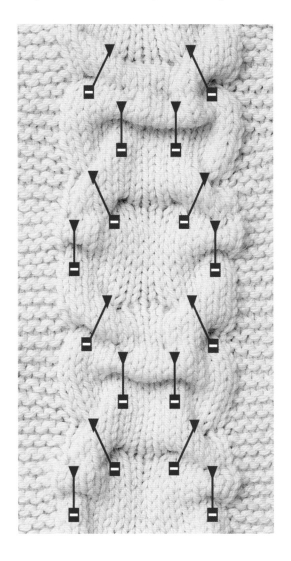

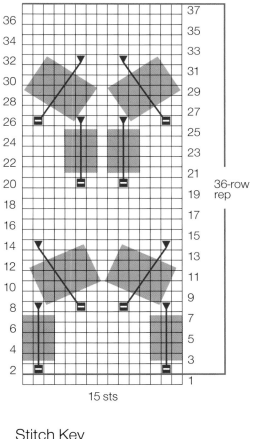

Stitch Key

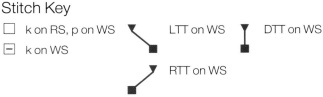

□ k on RS, p on WS   ▼ LTT on WS   ▮ DTT on WS

⊟ k on WS

▼ RTT on WS

23

NEEDLES

I recommend only using needles with long tapers and pointy tips. This will make it easier to pick up the Tuck Stitches and when knitting or purling multiple stitches together. Needle size should be paired appropriately with the yarn and for the desired gauge.

YARN CONSIDERATIONS

The most appropriate type of yarn to use for Dimensional Tuck Knitting is a *smooth, round, multi-plied* yarn. Yarns such as these are ideal because of their high degree of stitch definition and the cohesive fabric they create. An example of this type of yarn is Cascade 220®, which was used for all of the sample swatches in this book.

Smooth single-ply yarns, like their multi-ply siblings, can also be used successfully, the only drawback being that some single-plies may not be strong enough for a single Tuck Stitch to sustain the weight of its own fabric.

Yarns typically worked in a relatively loose gauge such as *mohairs, boucles, and highly-textured novelty* yarns can be used if extra considerations are made. As it may be difficult to locate Tuck Stitches among these textured yarns, you may want to insert a removable stitch marker into each Tuck Stitch as it is made. The markers make the Tuck Stitches easy to find when they need to be picked up. As these types of yarns benefit from a loose gauge to allow the texture of the yarn itself to fill in the negative space, the fabric produced might not have enough substance or volume to produce a Dimensional Tuck with great depth. Accordingly, when using yarns such as these an increase in the scale of the Dimensional Tucks is recommended (see Nature & Mechanics, Factor 3: Scale on page 13 for further discussion).

Chainette yarns must be thoroughly swatched before using. Chainettes can be stable and smooth, or they can be fuzzy and somewhat stretchy. I suggest inserting removable stitch markers into the Tuck Stitches with this type of yarn to eliminate the frustration of trying to find them among the fuzziness and to avoid snagging or splitting the yarn.

Thick-and-thin yarns can be appropriate if each thick or thin portion is relatively short and the difference between the thickest and thinnest sections is not too dramatic. Swatching is required to make sure that several rows of either section, thick or thin, do not stack on top of each other, otherwise the symmetry of the tucks could be lost.

Self-striping yarns with very long color sequences tend to work well with Dimensional Tuck stitch patterns while those with shorter color sequences can be problematic. Short color sequences can inadvertently allow colors to pool in distracting ways. They can also dazzle viewers with their quickly changing colors and pull attention away from the shape and form of the stitch pattern. Generally speaking, harmonious or tonal color palettes work better than those with high color contrast. That said, the inherent nature of Dimensional Tucks, which fold upon themselves, could overcome the problems of color pooling and viewer distraction. In the end, it all comes back to swatching and hoping for the best!

Hand-dyed yarns have their individual pros and cons and will vary with each unique colorist or dyer. Color Stacking is a technique I have found very well-suited to many Dimensional Tuck stitch patterns. Artful Color, Mindful Knits: The Definitive Guide to Working with Hand-dyed Yarn, by Laura Militzer Bryant, of Prism Yarns describes many color-stacking techniques that work exceptionally well with Dimensional Tucks.

TENSION

Dimensional Tucks are best worked in a gauge that creates an even, stable, and homogenous fabric. Your stitches should be secure enough that lifting a Tuck Stitch up to the needle will fold the fabric rather than dramatically stretch out the stitch.

Having said that, Dimensional Tucks can be used effectively with fine yarns in a looser gauge. For example, the Whisper Shawl (see pages 176–179) is worked with Rowan's *Kid Silk Haze* on size 10½ (6.5mm) needles. The fabric created is as expected for that yarn in that gauge—not extremely stable, with stitches easily snagged and pulled out of shape—and yet it works. The lightness of the

fabric—the weight of the fabric itself—does not pull unduly on the lifted Tuck Stitches, which allows the pattern to maintain its shape. Using a worsted or heavier weight yarn in a comparable gauge would create a fabric much too heavy. Dimension would be lost as the weight of the fabric itself would stretch out the Tuck Stitches and steal yarn from their neighbors.

Yarn Considerations (see previous page) discusses several types of yarns and how they can appropriately be used with Dimensional Tuck Knitting, but of course the ultimate tell-all regarding how your chosen yarn and gauge will behave is to work a swatch.

GAUGE

When swatching for a project that uses Dimensional Tucks, you should always begin with a simple stockinette swatch. This is important so you can confirm that you will be creating a fabric to your liking in regard to color, feel, and so forth. Next, whip up a test swatch in the Dimensional Tuck stitch pattern to find your gauge. Test swatches should be worked as follows:

For a single repeat of a stitch pattern, your swatch should have at least a few stitches of your chosen background stitch on each side, and it should be a minimum of 3 repeats in length. A swatch of this size will allow the folds to settle in place and not be distorted by the cast-on or bound-off edges.

If you intend to use a background stitch such as stockinette stitch which does not create an easily seen dividing line between the pattern and the background, it is recommended to use a marking thread at each of these boundaries as follows: After the first few rows of your swatch, insert a length of contrasting scrap yarn *between* the pattern stitches and the background stitches. Every two rows, alternate moving one end of the marking thread to the front or the back of your work. This will leave a trail of marking threads woven through your swatch.

For an allover stitch pattern, your swatch should be a minimum of 6 inches wide, not including your background stitch borders. It should also be a minimum of 4 repeats wide and 3 repeats long to allow the folds to settle into place.

Dimensional Tucks fold, bend, and double back on themselves. This deep texture makes it difficult to isolate a single horizontal row, measure the width, and count the stitches. There is an easy workaround: Take all measurements from the wrong side of the fabric. The wrong side is flatter than the right side, making it easier to measure without navigating over the various tucks.

Having the background stitch borders or marking threads in place, as suggested, serves two purposes. They indicate exactly where the stitch pattern begins and ends, and they help you take a truly horizontal measurement. Simply line up your ruler or tape measure across the pattern stitches from one easily seen background row to the same row on the other side of the stitch pattern, or from one marking thread to the other. The measurement taken in this manner will give you the most accurate pattern stitch gauge.

BLOCKING

For most applications, it is recommended to wet block Dimensional Tuck stitch patterns. Before soaking, gently tug the swatch both horizontally and vertically, from side to side and from top to bottom. This will ensure that the tucks are

well-seated. After a good long bath, fluff, pat, and pinch the fabric so the tucks stand in high relief. You should also make sure the edges of your background stitch are straight and are not stretched out.

RIBBONS,
CHAINS,
& LOOPS

1

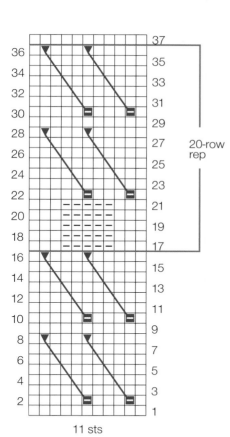

11 sts

20-row rep

1

Double Double Right Twist

(over 11 sts)

Row 1 and all RS rows thru row 15 Knit.

Row 2 P5, k1, p3, k1, p1.

Rows 4 and 6 Purl.

Row 8 P1, LTT, p3, LTT, p5.

Row 10 P5, k1, p3, k1, p1.

Rows 12 and 14 Purl.

Row 16 P1, LTT, p3, LTT, p5.

Rows 17, 19, and 21 K3, p5, k3.

Rows 18 and 20 P3, k5, p3.

Rows 22–36 Rep rows 2–16.

Rep rows 17–36 as many times as necessary.

Row 37 Knit.

Stitch Key

☐ k on RS, p on WS

⊟ p on RS, k on WS

▼ LTT on WS

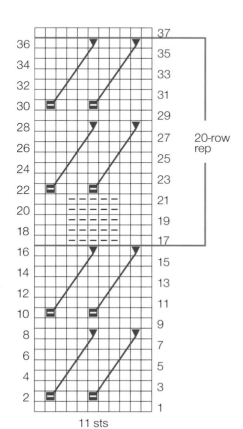

11 sts

20-row rep

2

Double Double Left Twist

(over 11 sts)

Row 1 and all RS rows thru row 15 Knit.

Row 2 P1, k1, p3, k1, p5.

Rows 4 and 6 Purl.

Row 8 P5, RTT, p3, RTT, p1.

Row 10 P1, k1, p3, k1, p5.

Rows 12 and 14 Purl.

Row 16 P5, RTT, p3, RTT, p1.

Rows 17, 19, and 21 K3, p5, k3.

Rows 18 and 20 P3, k5, p3.

Rows 22–36 Rep rows 2–16.

Rep rows 17–36 as many times as necessary.

Row 37 Knit.

Stitch Key

☐ k on RS, p on WS

⊟ p on RS, k on WS

▼ RTT on WS

3

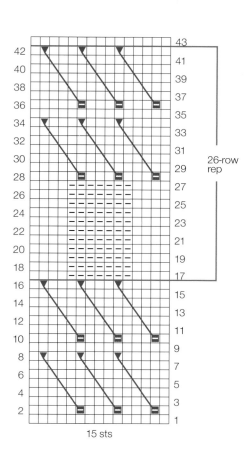

15 sts

3

Triple Double Right Twist

(over 15 sts)

Row 1 and all RS rows thru row 15 Knit.

Row 2 P5, k1, p3, k1, p3, k1, p1.

Rows 4 and 6 Purl.

Row 8 P1, LTT, p3, LTT, p3, LTT, p5.

Row 10 P5, k1, p3, k1, p3, k1, p1.

Rows 12 and 14 Purl.

Row 16 P1, LTT, p3, LTT, p3, LTT, p5.

Row 17 and all RS rows thru row 27 K4, p7, k4.

Row 18 and all WS rows thru row 26 P4, k7, p4.

Rows 28–42 Rep rows 2–16.

Rep rows 17–42 as many times as necessary.

Row 43 Knit.

Stitch Key

☐ k on RS, p on WS

⊟ p on RS, k on WS

▼ LTT on WS

26-row rep

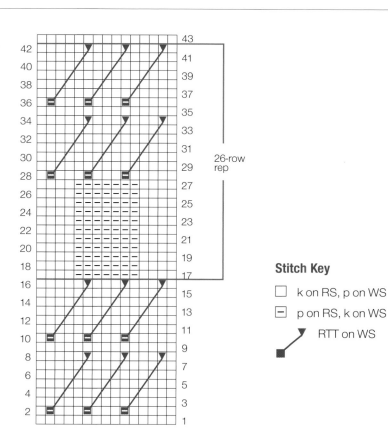

15 sts

4

Triple Double Left Twist

(over 15 sts)

Row 1 and all RS rows thru row 15 Knit.

Row 2 P1, k1, p3, k1, p3, k1, p5.

Rows 4 and 6 Purl.

Row 8 P5, RTT, p3, RTT, p3, RTT, p1.

Row 10 P1, k1, p3, k1, p3, k1, p5.

Rows 12 and 14 Purl.

Row 16 P5, RTT, p3, RTT, p3, RTT, p1.

Row 17 and all RS rows thru row 27 K4, p7, k4.

Row 18 and all WS rows thru row 26 P4, k7, p4.

Rows 28–42 Rep rows 2–16.

Rep rows 17–42 as many times as necessary.

Row 43 Knit.

Stitch Key

☐ k on RS, p on WS

⊟ p on RS, k on WS

▼ RTT on WS

26-row rep

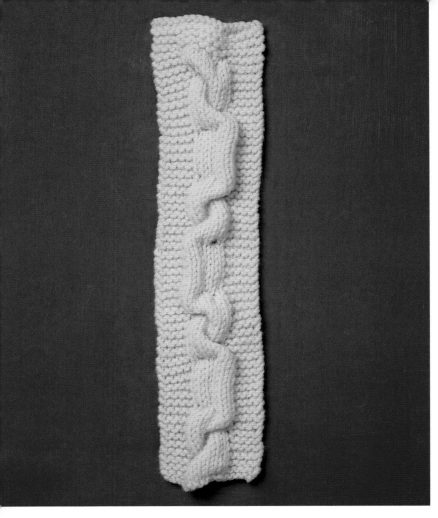

5

Spaced Alternating Twist

(over 7 sts)

Row 1 and all RS rows thru row 19 Knit.

Row 2 P5, k1, p1.

Rows 4 and 6 Purl.

Row 8 P1, LTT, p5.

Rows 10 and 12 Purl.

Row 14 P5, k1, p1.

Rows 16 and 18 Purl.

Row 20 P1, LTT, p5.

Rows 21, 23, 25, 27, 29, and 31 K3, p1, k3.

Rows 22, 24, 26, 28, and 30 P3, k1, p3.

Row 32 P1, k1, p5.

Rows 33, 35, and 37 Knit.

Rows 34 and 36 Purl.

Row 38 P5, RTT, p1.

Rows 39, 41, and 43 Knit.

Rows 40 and 42 Purl.

Row 44 P1, k1, p5.

Rows 45, 47, and 49 Knit.

Rows 46 and 48 Purl.

Row 50 P5, RTT, p1.

Rows 51–61 Rep rows 21–31.

Rep rows 2–61 as many times as necessary.

Rows 62–68 Rep rows 2–8.

Row 69 Knit.

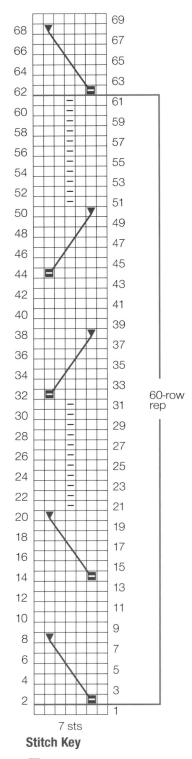

60-row rep

7 sts

Stitch Key

☐ k on RS, p on WS

⊟ p on RS, k on WS

▼ LTT on WS

▼ RTT on WS

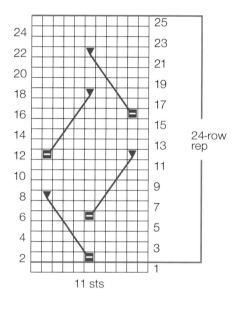

11 sts

Stitch Key

 k on RS, p on WS

 k on WS

LTT on WS

RTT on WS

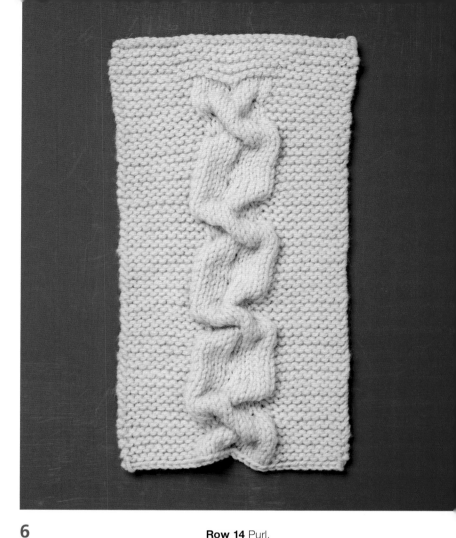

6

Tilted Chain

(over 11 sts)

Row 1 and all RS rows Knit.

Row 2 P5, k1, p5.

Row 4 Purl.

Row 6 P5, k1, p5.

Row 8 P1, LTT, p9.

Row 10 Purl.

Row 12 P1, k1, p7, RTT, p1.

Row 14 Purl.

Row 16 P9, k1, p1.

Row 18 P5, RTT, p5.

Row 20 Purl.

Row 22 P5, LTT, p5.

Row 24 Purl.

Row 25 Knit.

Rep rows 2–25.

33

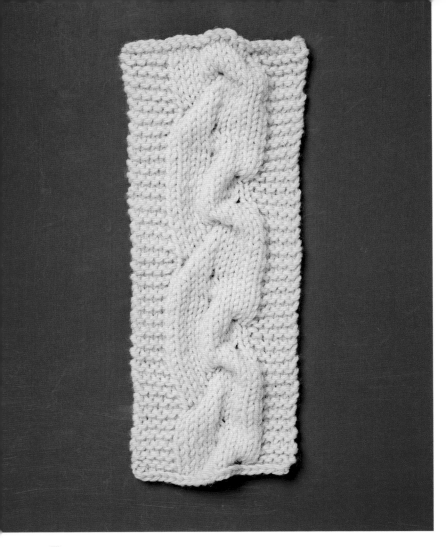

24-row rep

11 sts

7
Bunting

(over 11 sts)

Row 1 and all RS rows Knit.

Row 2 P9, k1, p1.

Rows 4, 8, 12, 16, 20, and 24 Purl.

Row 6 P5, LTT, p5.

Row 10 P5, k1, p5.

Row 14 P1, LTT, p9.

Row 18 P5, k1, p5.

Row 22 P9, RTT, p1.

Row 25 Knit.

Rep rows 2–25.

Stitch Key

☐ k on RS, p on WS

⊟ k on WS

LTT on WS

RTT on WS

Stitch Key

☐ k on RS, p on WS

⊟ k on WS

 LTT on WS

 RTT on WS

8
Kinked Chain

(over 11 sts)

Row 1 and all RS rows Knit.

Row 2 P1, k1, p9.

Row 4 P9, k1, p1.

Row 6 Purl.

Row 8 P5, RTT, p5.

Row 10 P5, LTT, p5.

Row 12 P5, k1, p5.

Rows 14 and 16 Purl.

Row 18 P1, LTT, p9.

Row 20 P9, k1, p1.

Row 22 P1, k1, p9.

Row 24 Purl.

Row 26 P5, LTT, p5.

Row 28 P5, RTT, p5.

Row 30 P5, k1, p5.

Rows 32 and 34 Purl.

Row 36 P9, RTT, p1.

Row 37 Knit.

Rep rows 2–37.

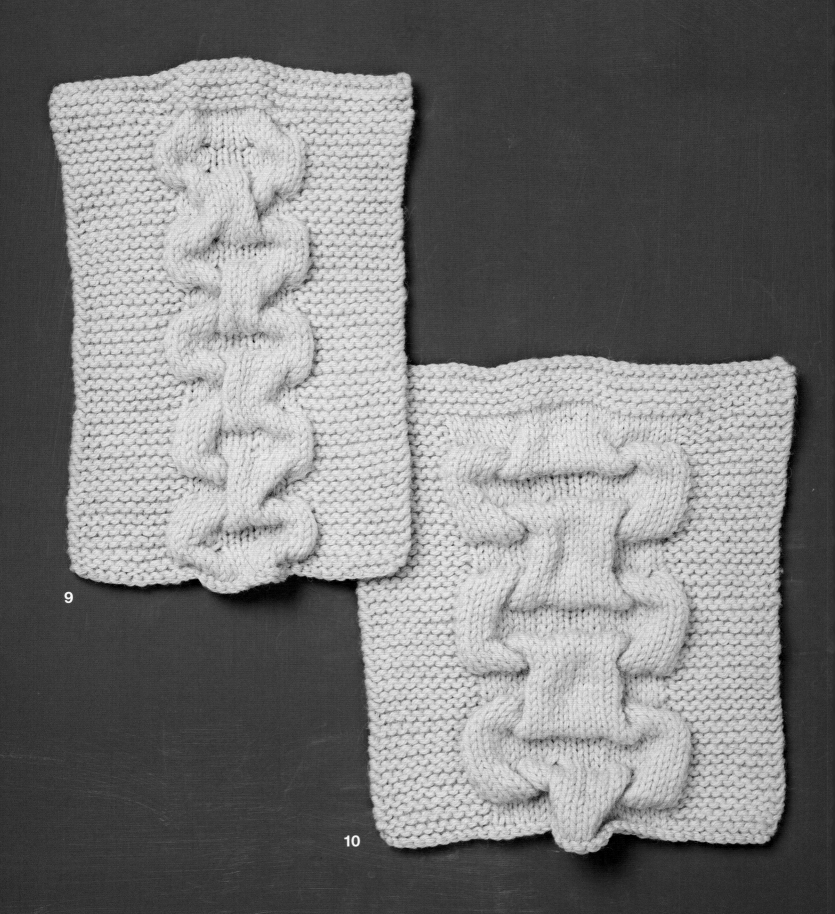

9

10

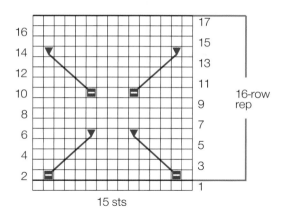

15 sts

16-row rep

Stitch Key

☐ k on RS, p on WS

⊟ k on WS

LTT on WS

RTT on WS

9
Chain Link

(over 15 sts)

Row 1 and all RS rows Knit.

Row 2 P1, k1, p11, k1, p1.

Row 4 Purl.

Row 6 P5, RTT, p3, LTT, p5.

Row 8 Purl.

Row 10 P5, k1, p3, k1, p5.

Row 12 Purl.

Row 14 P1, LTT, p11, RTT, p1.

Row 16 Purl.

Row 17 Knit.

Rep rows 2–17.

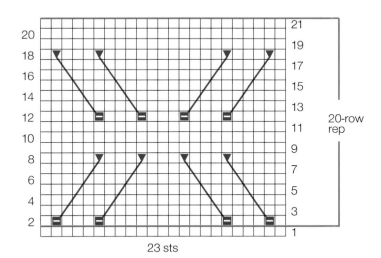

23 sts

20-row rep

Stitch Key

☐ k on RS, p on WS

⊟ k on WS

LTT on WS

RTT on WS

10
Double Chain Link

(over 23 sts)

Row 1 and all RS rows Knit.

Row 2 P1, k1, p3, k1, p11, k1, p3, k1, p1.

Rows 4 and 6 Purl.

Row 8 P5, RTT, p3, RTT, p3, LTT, p3, LTT, p5.

Row 10 Purl.

Row 12 P5, k1, p3, k1, p3, k1, p3, k1, p5.

Rows 14 and 16 Purl.

Row 18 P1, LTT, p3, LTT, p11, RTT, p3, RTT, p1.

Row 20 Purl.

Row 21 Knit.

Rep rows 2–21.

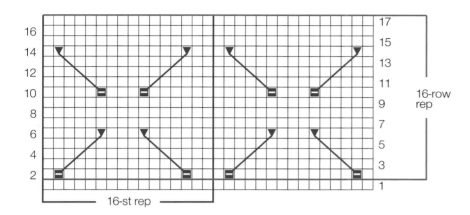

Stitch Key

	k on RS, p on WS
−	k on WS
▼	LTT on WS
▼	RTT on WS

11

Chain Link Panel

(multiple of 16 sts plus 15 sts)

Row 1 and all RS rows Knit.

Row 2 *P1, k1, p11, k1, p2; rep from * to last 15 sts, p1, k1, p11, k1, p1.

Row 4 Purl.

Row 6 *P5, RTT, p3, LTT, p6; rep from * to last 15 sts, p5, RTT, p3, LTT, p5.

Row 8 Purl.

Row 10 *P5, k1, p3, k1, p6; rep from * to last 15 sts, p5, k1, p3, k1, p5.

Row 12 Purl.

Row 14 *P1, LTT, p11, RTT, p2; rep from * to last 15 sts, p1, LTT, p11, RTT, p1.

Row 16 Purl.

Row 17 Knit.

Rep rows 2–17.

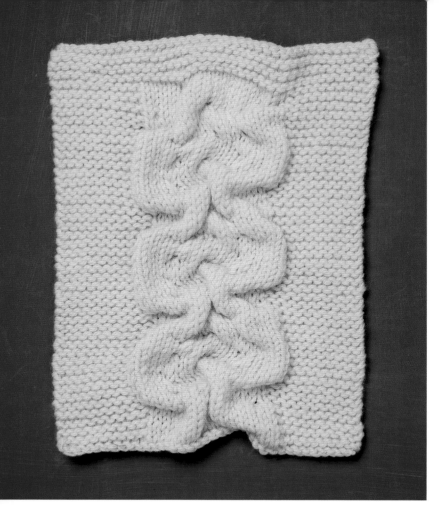

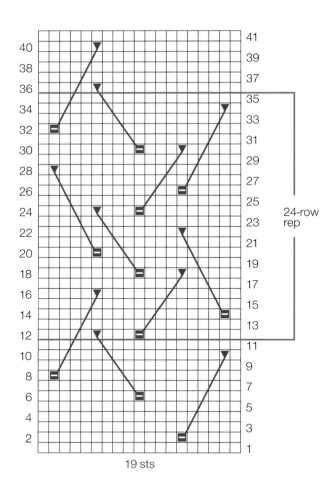

12
Staggered Loops

(over 19 sts)

Row 1 and all RS rows Knit.

Row 2 P13, k1, p5.

Row 4 Purl.

Row 6 P9, k1, p9.

Row 8 P1, k1, p17.

Row 10 P17, RTT, p1.

Row 12 P5, LTT, p3, k1, p9.

Row 14 P17, k1, p1.

Row 16 P5, RTT, p13.

Row 18 P9, k1, p3, RTT, p5.

Row 20 P5, k1, p13.

Row 22 P13, LTT, p5.

Row 24 P5, LTT, p3, k1, p9.

Row 26 P13, k1, p5.

Row 28 P1, LTT, p17.

Row 30 P9, k1, p3, RTT, p5.

Row 32 P1, k1, p17.

Row 34 P17, RTT, p1.

Row 35 Knit.

Rep rows 12–35 as many times as

necessary.

Row 36 P5, LTT, P13.

Row 38 Purl.

Row 40 P5, RTT, P13.

Row 41 Knit.

Stitch Key

☐ k on RS, p on WS

⊟ k on WS

▼ LTT on WS

■

▼ RTT on WS

■

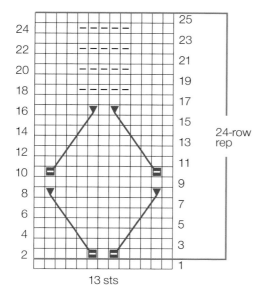

13 sts

Stitch Key

☐ k on RS, p on WS

⊟ k on WS

◥ LTT on WS

◥ RTT on WS

13

Long Chain with Center Garter

(over 13 sts)

Row 1 and all RS rows Knit.

Row 2 P5, k1, p1, k1, p5.

Rows 4 and 6 Purl.

Row 8 P1, LTT, p9, RTT, p1.

Row 10 P1, k1, p9, k1, p1.

Rows 12 and 14 Purl.

Row 16 P5, RTT, p1, LTT, p5.

Rows 18, 20, 22, and 24 P4, k5, p4.

Row 25 Knit.

Rep rows 2–25.

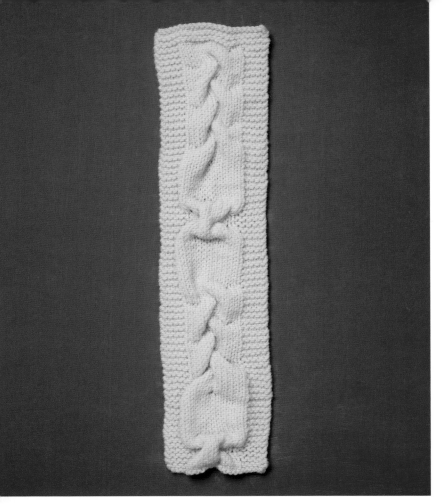

14

Three Linked Braids

(over 13 sts)

Row 1 and all RS rows Knit.

Row 2 P5, k1, p1, k1, p5.

Row 4 Purl.

Row 6 P1, LTT, p9, RTT, p1.

Row 8 Purl.

Row 10 P1, k1, p9, k1, p1.

Row 12 Purl.

Row 14 P5, RTT, p1, LTT, p5.

Rows 16, 18, 20, 22, and 24 Purl.

Row 26 P6, k1, p6.

Rows 28 and 30 Purl.

Row 32 P2, LTT, p3, k1, p6.

Rows 34 and 36 Purl.

Row 38 P6, k1, p3, RTT, p2.

Rows 40 and 42 Purl.

Row 44 P2, LTT, p3, k1, p6.

Rows 46 and 48 Purl.

Row 50 P6, k1, p3, RTT, p2.

Rows 52 and 54 Purl.

Row 56 P2, LTT, p3, k1, p6.

Rows 58 and 60 Purl.

Row 62 P10, RTT, p2.

Rows 64, 66, 68, 70, and 72 Purl.

Row 73 Knit.

Rep rows 2–73.

Stitch Key

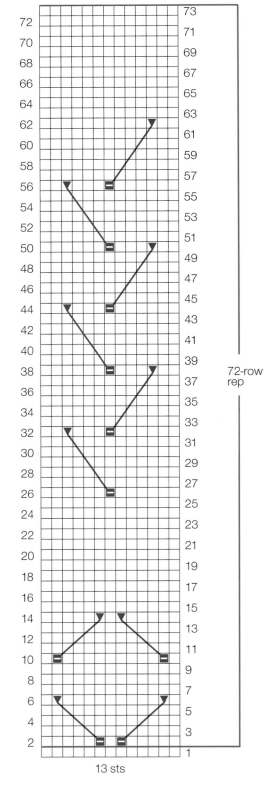

□ k on RS, p on WS

⊟ k on WS

⬛↘ LTT on WS

↘⬛ RTT on WS

72-row rep

13 sts

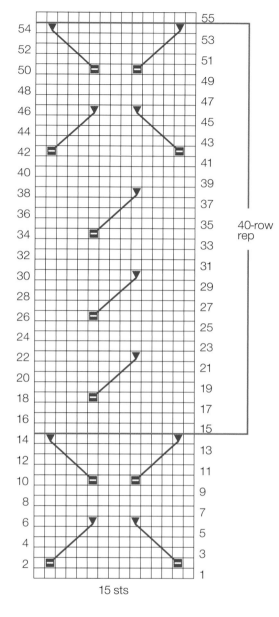

15 sts

Stitch Key

☐ k on RS, p on WS

⊟ k on WS

 LTT on WS

 RTT on WS

15

Twists with Diamonds

(over 15 sts)

Row 1 and all RS rows Knit.

Row 2 P1, k1, p11, k1, p1.

Row 4 Purl.

Row 6 P5, RTT, p3, LTT, p5.

Row 8 Purl.

Row 10 P5, k1, p3, k1, p5.

Row 12 Purl.

Row 14 P1, LTT, p11, RTT, p1.

Row 16 Purl.

Row 18 P5, k1, p9.

Row 20 Purl.

Row 22 P9, RTT, p5.

Row 24 Purl.

Row 26 P5, k1, p9.

Row 28 Purl.

Row 30 P9, RTT, p5.

Row 32 Purl.

Row 34 P5, k1, p9.

Row 36 Purl.

Row 38 P9, RTT, p5.

Row 40 Purl.

Row 41 Knit.

Rows 42–54 Rep rows 2–14.

Rep rows 15–54 as many times as

necessary.

Row 55 Knit.

43

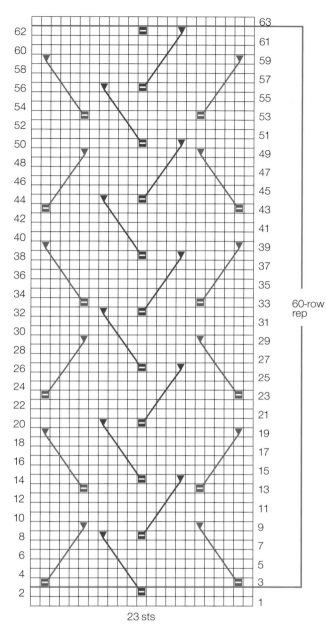

```
62                          ▬      ◣           63
60    ◣                              ◢          61
58        ◣                      ◢              59
56            ◣      ▬      ◢                   57
54              ▬          ▬                    55
52                  ◢      ◣                    53
50                      ▬                       51
48                  ◢          ◣               49
46                                             47
44          ▬      ◣              ◣      ▬      45
42                                             43
40    ◣              ◢                          41
38              ◣      ▬      ◢                  39
36                                             37
34              ▬          ▬                    35
32                  ◣      ◢                    33
30        ◢                      ◣              31
28                                             29
26                  ◣      ◢                    27
24    ▬                              ▬          25
22                                             23
20    ◣              ◢                          21
18              ◣      ▬      ◢                  19
16                                             17
14              ▬          ▬                    15
12                  ◢      ◣                    13
10        ◢                      ◣              11
 8              ◢      ▬      ◣                  9
 6                                              7
 4    ▬              ▬              ▬           5
 2                                              3
                                                1
```

23 sts

Stitch Key

☐ k on RS, p on WS

⊟ p on RS, k on WS

◥ LTT on WS

◢ RTT on WS

◥ RTT from WS

◢ LTT from WS

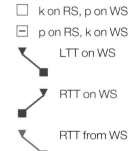

16

Center Braid with Loops

(over 23 sts)

Note This pattern uses two methods of Dimensional Tucks. In the chart, LTT from WS and RTT from WS appear in red to help differentiate them from LTT on WS and RTT on WS.

Row 1 (RS) Knit.

Row 2 P11, k1, p11.

Row 3 K1, p1, k19, p1, k1.

Rows 4 and 6 Purl.

Rows 5 and 7 Knit.

Row 8 (WS) P7, LTT, p3, k1, p11.

Row 9 (RS) K5, RTT, k11, LTT, k5.

Rows 10 and 12 Purl.

Row 11 Knit.

Row 13 K5, p1, k11, p1, k5.

Row 14 (WS) P11, k1, p3, RTT, p7.

Rows 15 and 17 Knit.

Rows 16 and 18 Purl.

Row 19 (RS) K1, LTT, k19, RTT, k1.

Row 20 (WS) P7, LTT, p3, k1, p11.

Row 21 Knit.

Row 22 Purl.

Row 23 K1, p1, k19, p1, k1.

Row 24 Purl.

Row 25 Knit.

Row 26 (WS) P11, k1, p3, RTT, p7.

Row 27 Knit.

Row 28 Purl.

Row 29 (RS) K5, RTT, k11, LTT, k5.

Row 30 Purl.

Row 31 Knit.

Row 32 (WS) P7, LTT, p3, k1, p11.

Row 33 K5, p1, k11, p1, k5.

Rows 34 and 36 Purl.

Rows 35 and 37 Knit.

Row 38 (WS) P11, k1, p3, RTT, p7.

Row 39 (RS) K1, LTT, k19, RTT, k1.

Rows 40 and 42 Purl.

Row 41 Knit.

Row 43 K1, p1, k19, p1, k1.

Row 44 (WS) P7, LTT, p3, k1, p11.

Rows 45 and 47 Knit.

Rows 46 and 48 Purl.

Row 49 (RS) K5, RTT, k11, LTT, k5.

Row 50 (WS) P11, k1, p3, RTT, p7.

Row 51 Knit.

Row 52 Purl.

Row 53 K5, p1, k11, p1, k5.

Row 54 Purl.

Row 55 Knit.

Row 56 (WS) P7, LTT, p3, k1, p11.

Row 57 Knit.

Row 58 Purl.

Row 59 (RS) K1, LTT, k19, RTT, k1.

Row 60 Purl.

Row 61 Knit.

Row 62 (WS) P11, k1, p3, RTT, p7.

Rep rows 3–62 as many times as necessary, omitting the knit Tuck Stitch on final row 62.

Row 63 Knit.

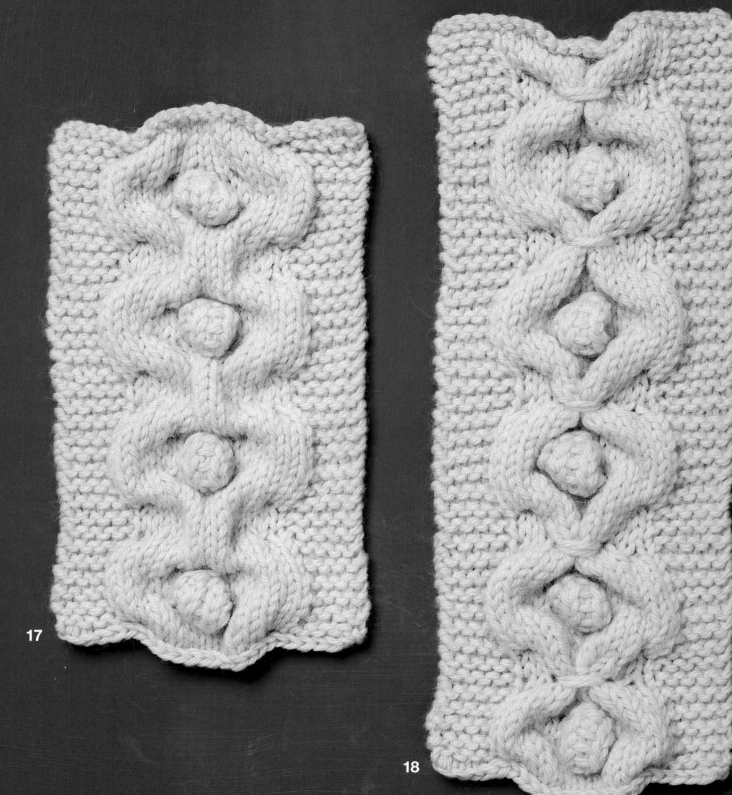

17

18

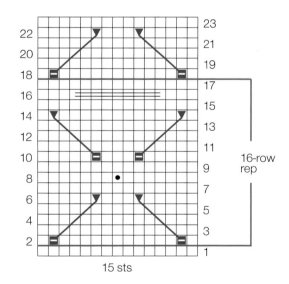

Stitch Key

□ k on RS, p on WS
─ k on WS
⊡ MB

◤ LTT on WS

◥ RTT on WS

17
Bobbled Chains
(over 15 sts)

MB (make bobble) M1, yo, kfb, yo, M1, [sl 6 sts from RH needle to LH needle as foll: (sl 1 wyib, sl 1 wyif) 3 times; p6] 4 times, sl 6 sts from RH needle to LH needle as foll: (sl 1 wyib, sl 1 wyif) 3 times; [p3tog] twice, pass first st over 2nd st and off needle.

Row 1 and all RS rows Knit.

Row 2 P1, k1, p11, k1, p1.

Row 4 Purl.

Row 6 P5, RTT, p3, LTT, p5.

Row 8 P7, MB, p7.

Row 10 P5, k1, p3, k1, p5.

Row 12 Purl.

Row 14 P1, LTT, p11, RTT, p1.

Row 16 Purl.

Row 17 Knit.

Rep rows 2–17 as many times as necessary.

Rows 18–22 Rep rows 2–6.

Row 23 Knit.

Stitch Key

□ k on RS, p on WS
─ k on WS
⊡ MB

◤ LTT on WS

◥ RTT on WS

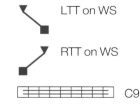 C9

18
Cinched Bobbled Chains
(over 15 sts)

MB (make bobble) M1, yo, kfb, yo, M1, [sl 6 sts from RH needle to LH needle as foll: (sl 1 wyib, sl 1 wyif) 3 times; p6] 4 times, sl 6 sts from RH needle to LH needle as foll: (sl 1 wyib, sl 1 wyif) 3 times; [p3tog] twice, pass first st over 2nd st and off needle.

C9 (cinch 9) [Wyib sl 9 sts to RH needle, wyif sl 9 sts to LH needle] twice, pull yarn snug to cinch.

Row 1 and all RS rows Knit.

Row 2 P1, k1, p11, k1, p1.

Row 4 Purl.

Row 6 P5, RTT, p3, LTT, p5.

Row 8 P7, MB, p7.

Row 10 P5, k1, p3, k1, p5.

Row 12 Purl.

Row 14 P1, LTT, p11, RTT, p1.

Row 16 P3, C9, p9 (cinched sts), p3.

Row 17 Knit.

Rep rows 2–17 as many times as necessary.

Rows 18–22 Rep rows 2–6.

Row 23 Knit.

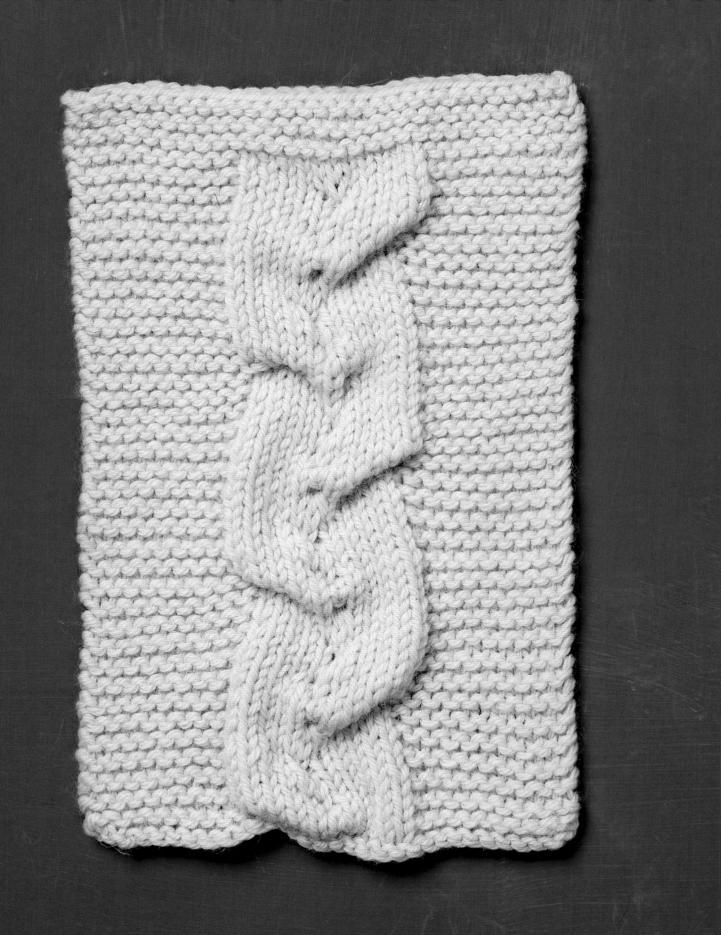

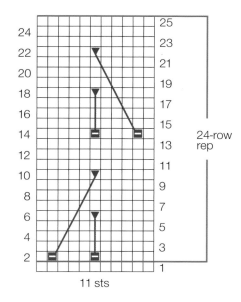

11 sts

24-row rep

Stitch Key

☐ k on RS, p on WS

⊟ k on WS

LTT on WS

RTT on WS

DTT on WS

19
Gathered Ribbon

(over 11 sts)

Row 1 and all RS rows Knit.

Row 2 P1, k1, p3, k1, p5.

Row 4 Purl.

Row 6 P5, DTT, p5.

Row 8 Purl.

Row 10 P5, RTT, p5.

Row 12 Purl.

Row 14 P5, k1, p3, k1, p1.

Row 16 Purl.

Row 18 P5, DTT, p5.

Row 20 Purl.

Row 22 P5, LTT, p5.

Row 24 Purl.

Row 25 Knit.

Rep rows 2–25.

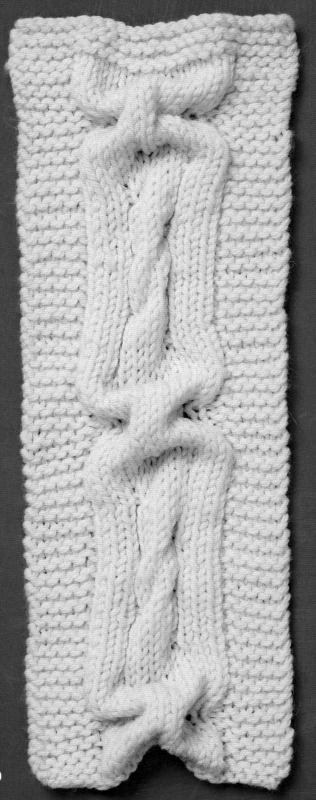

20

21

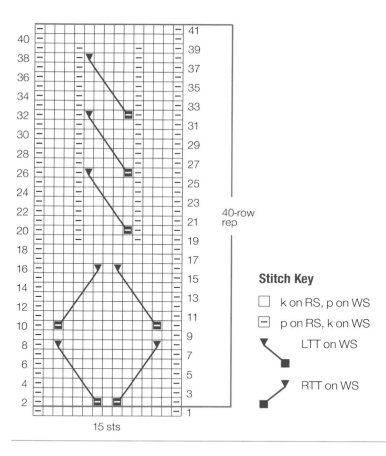

20

Long Chain with 3 Right Twists

(over 15 sts)

Row 1 and all RS rows thru row 17 P1, k13, p1.

Row 2 K1, p5, k1, p1, k1, p5, k1.

Rows 4 and 6 K1, p13, k1.

Row 8 K1, p1, LTT, p9, RTT, p1, k1.

Row 10 K1, p1, k1, p9, k1, p1, k1.

Rows 12 and 14 K1, p13, k1.

Row 16 K1, p5, RTT, p1, LTT, p5, k1.

Row 18 K1, p13, k1.

Row 19 and all RS rows thru row 39 P1, k3, p1, k5, p1, k3, p1.

Row 20 K1, p3, k1, p4, k2, p3, k1.

Rows 22 and 24 K1, p3, k1, p5, k1, p3, k1.

Row 26 K1, p3, k1, LTT, p3, k2, p3, k1.

Rows 28 and 30 K1, p3, k1, p5, k1, p3, k1.

Row 32 K1, p3, k1, LTT, p3, k2, p3, k1.

Rows 34 and 36 K1, p3, k1, p5, k1, p3, k1.

Row 38 K1, p3, k1, LTT, p4, k1, p3, k1.

Row 40 K1, p13, k1.

Row 41 P1, k13, p1.

Rep rows 2–41.

Stitch Key

☐ k on RS, p on WS

⊟ p on RS, k on WS

LTT on WS

RTT on WS

15 sts

40-row rep

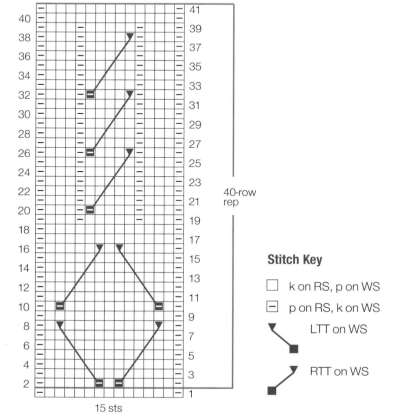

21

Long Chain with 3 Left Twists

(over 15 sts)

Row 1 and all RS rows thru row 17 P1, k13, p1.

Row 2 K1, p5, k1, p1, k1, p5, k1.

Rows 4 and 6 K1, p13, k1.

Row 8 K1, p1, LTT, p9, RTT, p1, k1.

Row 10 K1, p1, k1, p9, k1, p1, k1.

Rows 12 and 14 K1, p13, k1.

Row 16 K1, p5, RTT, p1, LTT, p5, k1.

Row 18 K1, p13, k1.

Row 19 and all RS rows thru row 39 P1, k3, p1, k5, p1, k3, p1.

Row 20 K1, p3, k2, p4, k1, p3, k1.

Rows 22 and 24 K1, p3, k1, p5, k1, p3, k1.

Row 26 K1, p3, k2, p3, RTT, k1, p3, k1.

Rows 28 and 30 K1, p3, k1, p5, k1, p3, k1.

Row 32 K1, p3, k2, p3, RTT, k1, p3, k1.

Rows 34 and 36 K1, p3, k1, p5, k1, p3, k1.

Row 38 K1, p3, k1, p4, RTT, k1, p3, k1.

Row 40 K1, p13, k1.

Row 41 P1, k13, p1.

Rep rows 2–41.

Stitch Key

☐ k on RS, p on WS

⊟ p on RS, k on WS

LTT on WS

RTT on WS

15 sts

40-row rep

22

23

22
Flame

(over 11 sts)

Note This swatch uses the alternate ON RS method while #23 Smoke (below) uses the standard ON WS method. Compare the two swatches for an example of the difference in appearance between the same Dimensional Tuck worked using two different methods.

Row 1 (RS) K1, p1, k7, p1, k1.

Row 2 and all WS rows Purl.

Rows 3 and 5 Knit.

Row 7 (RS) K5, LRTT, k5.

Rows 9 and 11 Knit.

Row 12 Purl.

Rep rows 1–12.

11 sts

12-row rep

Stitch Key

☐ k on RS, p on WS

⊟ p on RS

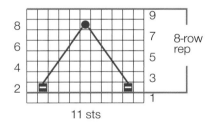 LRTT on RS

23
Smoke

(over 11 sts)

Row 1 and all RS rows Knit.

Row 2 P1, k1, p7, k1, p1.

Rows 4 and 6 Purl.

Row 8 P5, LRTT, p5.

Row 9 Knit.

Rep rows 2–9.

11 sts

8-row rep

Stitch Key

☐ k on RS, p on WS

⊟ k on WS

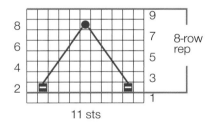 LRTT on WS

RIPPLES,
WAVES,
& CHEVRONS

24

25

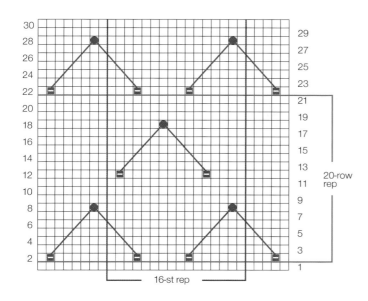

Stitch Key

☐ k on RS, p on WS

⊟ k on WS

 LRTT on WS

24
Lyre Panel

(multiple of 16 sts plus 13 sts)

Row 1 and all RS rows Knit.

Row 2 P1, k1, p6, *p3, k1, p5, k1, p6; rep from * to last 5 sts, p3, k1, p1.

Rows 4 and 6 Purl.

Row 8 P6, LRTT, p1, *p14, LRTT, p1; rep from * to last 5 sts, p5.

Row 10 Purl.

Row 12 P8, *p1, k1, p9, k1, p4; rep from * to last 5 sts, p5.

Rows 14 and 16 Purl.

Row 18 P8, *p6, LRTT, p9; rep from * to last 5 sts, p5.

Row 20 Purl.

Row 21 Knit.

Rep rows 2–21 as many times as necessary.

Rows 22–29 Rep rows 2–9.

Row 30 Purl.

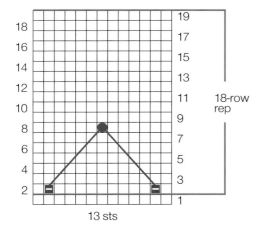

Stitch Key

☐ k on RS, p on WS

⊟ k on WS

 LRTT on WS

25
Lyre

(over 13 sts)

Row 1 and all RS rows Knit.

Row 2 P1, k1, p9, k1, p1.

Rows 4 and 6 Purl.

Row 8 P6, LRTT, p6.

Rows 10, 12, 14, 16, and 18 Purl.

Row 19 Knit.

Rep rows 2–19.

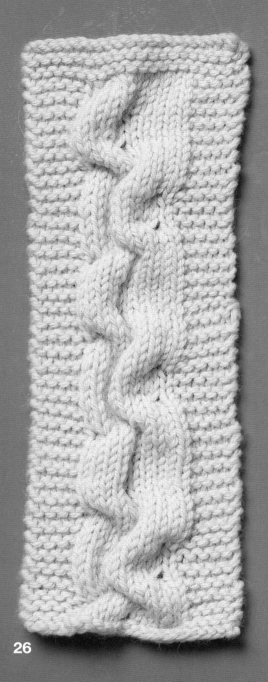

26

27

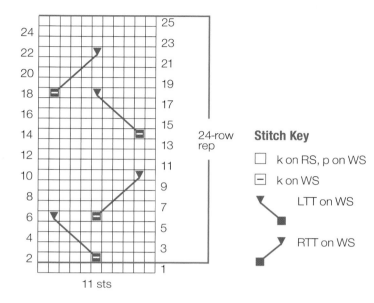

11 sts

24-row rep

Stitch Key

☐ k on RS, p on WS

⊟ k on WS

▼ LTT on WS

▼ RTT on WS

26
Rightward Dune

(over 11 sts)

Row 1 and all RS rows Knit.

Row 2 P5, k1, p5.

Row 4 Purl.

Row 6 P1, LTT, p3, k1, p5.

Row 8 Purl.

Row 10 P9, RTT, p1.

Row 12 Purl.

Row 14 P9, k1, p1.

Row 16 Purl.

Row 18 P1, k1, p3, LTT, p5.

Row 20 Purl.

Row 22 P5, RTT, p5.

Row 24 Purl.

Row 25 Knit.

Rep rows 2–25.

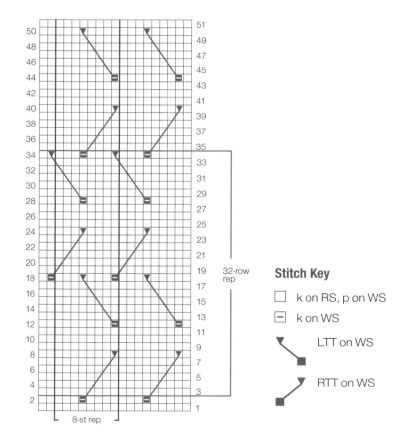

8-st rep

32-row rep

Stitch Key

☐ k on RS, p on WS

⊟ k on WS

▼ LTT on WS

▼ RTT on WS

27
Rightward Dune Panel

(multiple of 8 sts plus 11 sts)

Row 1 and all RS rows Knit.

Row 2 P2, *p3, k1, p4; rep from * to last 9 sts, p3, k1, p5.

Rows 4 and 6 Purl.

Row 8 P2, *p7, RTT; rep from * to last 9 sts, p7, RTT, p1.

Row 10 Purl.

Row 12 P2, *p7, k1; rep from * to last 9 sts, p7, k1, p1.

Rows 14 and 16 Purl.

Row 18 P1, k1, *p3, LTT, p3, k1; rep from * to last 9 sts, p3, LTT, p5.

Rows 20 and 22 Purl.

Row 24 P2, *p3, RTT, p4; rep from * to last 9 sts, p3, RTT, p5.

Row 26 Purl.

Row 28 P2, *p3, k1, p4; rep from * to last 9 sts, p3, k1, p5.

Rows 30 and 32 Purl.

Row 34 P1, LTT, *p3, k1, p3, LTT; rep from * to last 9 sts, p3, k1, p5.

Rep rows 3–34 as many times as necessary.

Rows 35–49 Rep rows 3–17.

Row 50 P2, *p3, LTT, p4; rep from * to last 9 sts, p3, LTT, p5.

Row 51 Knit.

28

Leftward Dune

(over 11 sts)

Row 1 and all RS rows Knit.

Row 2 P5, k1, p5.

Row 4 Purl.

Row 6 P5, k1, p3, RTT, p1.

Row 8 Purl.

Row 10 P1, LTT, p9.

Row 12 Purl.

Row 14 P1, k1, p9.

Row 16 Purl.

Row 18 P5, RTT, p3, k1, p1.

Row 20 Purl.

Row 22 P5, LTT, p5.

Row 24 Purl.

Row 25 Knit.

Rep rows 2–25.

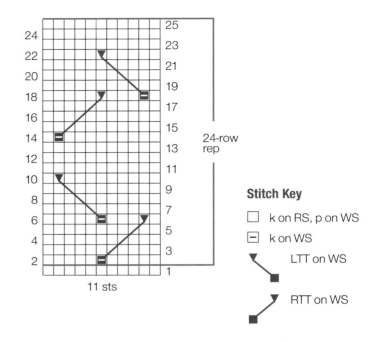

24-row rep

11 sts

Stitch Key

☐ k on RS, p on WS

⊟ k on WS

▼ LTT on WS

▼ RTT on WS

29

Leftward Dune Panel

(multiple of 8 sts plus 11 sts)

Row 1 and all RS rows Knit.

Row 2 P2, *p3, k1, p4; rep from * to last 9 sts, p3, k1, p5.

Rows 4 and 6 Purl.

Row 8 P1, LTT, *p7, LTT; rep from * to last 9 sts, p9.

Row 10 Purl.

Row 12 P1, k1, *p7, k1; rep from * to last 9 sts, p9.

Rows 14 and 16 Purl.

Row 18 P2, *p3, RTT, p3, k1; rep from * to last 9 sts, p3, RTT, p3, k1, p1.

Rows 20 and 22 Purl.

Row 24 P2, *p3, LTT, p4; rep from * to last 9 sts, p3, LTT, p5.

Row 26 Purl.

Row 28 P2, *p3, k1, p4; rep from * to last 9 sts, p3, k1, p5.

Rows 30 and 32 Purl.

Row 34 P2, *k3, k1, p3, RTT; rep from * to last 9 sts, p3, k1, p3, RTT, p1.

Rep rows 3–34 as many times as necessary.

Rows 35–49 Rep rows 3–17.

Row 50 P2, *p3, RTT, p4; rep from * to last 9 sts, p3, RTT, p5.

Row 51 Knit.

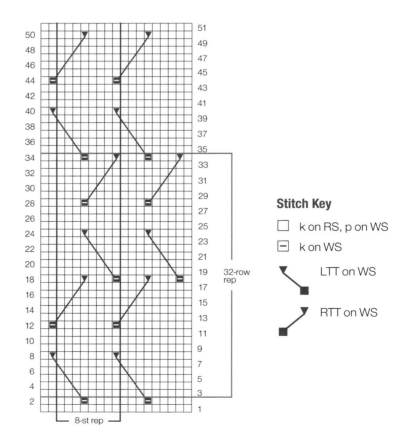

32-row rep

8-st rep

Stitch Key

☐ k on RS, p on WS

⊟ k on WS

▼ LTT on WS

▼ RTT on WS

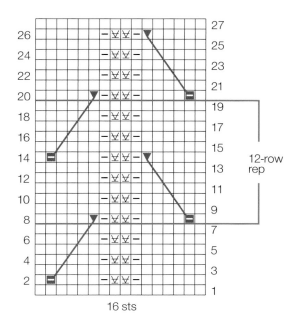

26
24
22
20
18
16
14
12
10
8
6
4
2

27
25
23
21
19
17
15
13
11
9
7
5
3
1

12-row
rep

16 sts

Stitch Key

☐ k on RS, p on WS

⊟ k on WS

⊻ sl 1 wyif

 LTT on WS

 RTT on WS

30

Wavy Braid with Center

(over 16 sts)

Row 1 and all RS rows Knit.

Row 2 P1, k1, p4, k1, sl 2 wyif, k1, p6.

Rows 4 and 6 P6, k1, sl 2 wyif, k1, p6.

Row 8 P5, RTT, k1, sl 2 wyif, k1, p4, k1, p1.

Rows 10 and 12 P6, k1, sl 2 wyif, k1, p6.

Row 14 P1, k1, p4, k1, sl 2 wyif, k1, LTT, p5.

Rows 16 and 18 P6, k1, sl 2 wyif, k1, p6.

Row 19 Knit.

Rep rows 8–19 as many times as necessary.

Rows 20–25 Rep rows 8–13.

Row 26 P6, k1, sl 2 wyif, k1, LTT, p5.

Row 27 Knit.

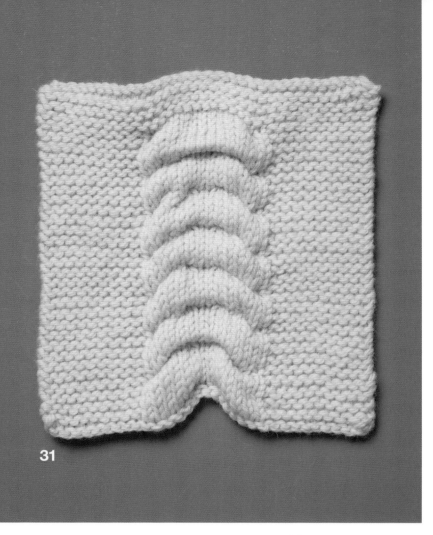

31

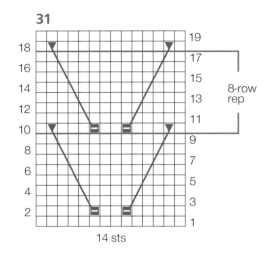

Stitch Key

☐ k on RS, p on WS

⊟ k on WS

LTT on WS

RTT on WS

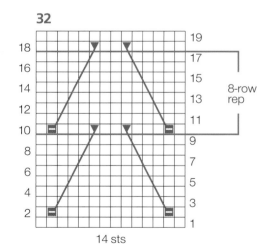

31

Downward Nestled Shells

(over 14 sts)

Row 1 and all RS rows Knit.

Row 2 P5, k1, p2, k1, p5.

Rows 4, 6, and 8 Purl.

Row 10 P1, LTT, p3, k1, p2, k1, p3, RTT, p1.

Rows 12, 14, and 16 Purl.

Row 17 Knit.

Rep rows 10–17 as many times as necessary.

Row 18 P1, LTT, p10, RTT, p1.

Row 19 Knit.

32

Upward Nestled Shells

(over 14 sts)

Row 1 and all RS rows Knit.

Row 2 P1, k1, p10, k1, p1.

Rows 4, 6, and 8 Purl.

Row 10 P1, k1, p3, RTT, p2, LTT, p3, k1, p1.

Rows 12, 14, and 16 Purl.

Row 17 Knit.

Rep rows 10–17 as many times as necessary.

Row 18 P5, RTT, p2, LTT, p5.

Row 19 Knit.

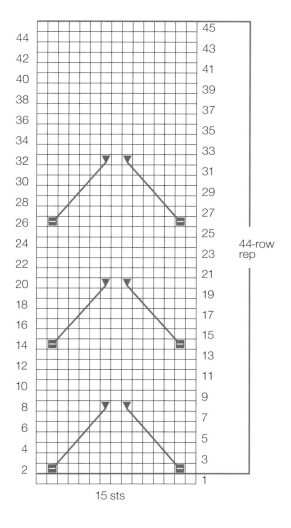

44-row rep

15 sts

Stitch Key

☐ k on RS, p on WS

⊟ k on WS

 LTT on WS

RTT on WS

33
Linked Chevrons

(over 15 sts)

Row 1 and all RS rows Knit.

Row 2 P1, k1, p11, k1, p1.

Rows 4 and 6 Purl.

Row 8 P6, RTT, p1, LTT, p6.

Rows 10 and 12 Purl.

Row 14 P1, k1, p11, k1, p1.

Rows 16 and 18 Purl.

Row 20 P6, RTT, p1, LTT, p6.

Rows 22 and 24 Purl.

Row 26 P1, k1, p11, k1, p1.

Rows 28 and 30 Purl.

Row 32 P6, RTT, p1, LTT, p6.

Rows 34, 36, 38, 40, 42, and 44

Purl.

Row 45 Knit.

Rep rows 2–45.

34

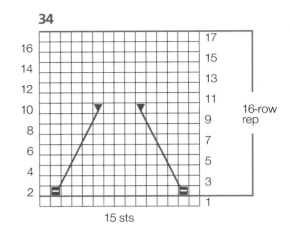

34

16-row rep

Stitch Key

☐ k on RS, p on WS

⊟ k on WS

▼ LTT on WS

▲ RTT on WS

34

Upward Horseshoe

(over 15 sts)

Row 1 and all RS rows Knit.

Row 2 P1, k1, p11, k1, p1.

Rows 4, 6, and 8 Purl.

Row 10 P5, RTT, p3, LTT, p5.

Rows 12, 14, and 16 Purl.

Row 17 Knit.

Rep rows 2–17.

35

Downward Horseshoe

(over 15 sts)

Row 1 and all RS rows Knit.

Row 2 P5, k1, p3, k1, p5.

Rows 4, 6, and 8 Purl.

Row 10 P1, LTT, p11, RTT, p1.

Rows 12, 14, and 16 Purl.

Row 17 Knit.

Rep rows 2–17.

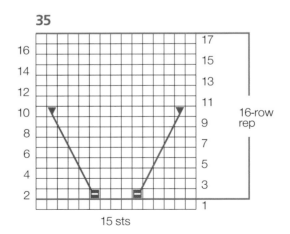

35

15 sts

16-row rep

36

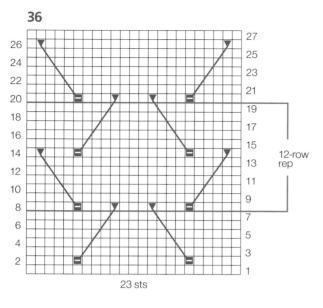

23 sts

Stitch Key

☐ k on RS, p on WS

⊟ k on WS

▼ LTT on WS

▶ RTT on WS

37

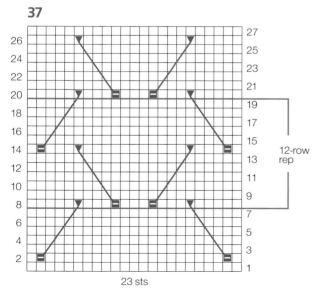

23 sts

36

Upward Shells with Twists

(over 23 sts)

Row 1 and all RS rows Knit.

Row 2 P5, k1, p11, k1, p5.

Rows 4 and 6 Purl.

Row 8 P5, k1, p3, RTT, p3, LTT, p3, k1, p5.

Rows 10 and 12 Purl.

Row 14 P1, LTT, p3, k1, p11, k1, p3, RTT, p1.

Rows 16 and 18 Purl.

Row 19 Knit.

Rep rows 8–19 as many times as necessary.

Rows 20–25 Rep rows 8–13.

Row 26 P1, LTT, p19, RTT, p1.

Row 27 Knit.

37

Downward Shells with Twists

(over 23 sts)

Row 1 and all RS rows Knit.

Row 2 P1, k1, p19, k1, p1.

Rows 4 and 6 Purl.

Row 8 P5, RTT, p3, k1, p3, k1, p3, LTT, p5.

Rows 10 and 12 Purl.

Row 14 P1, k1, p3, LTT, p11, RTT, p3, k1, p1.

Rows 16 and 18 Purl.

Row 19 Knit.

Rep rows 8–19 as many times as necessary.

Rows 20–25 Rep rows 8–13.

Row 26 P5, LTT, p11, RTT, p5.

Row 27 Knit.

RIPPLES, WAVES, & CHEVRONS

65

38

40

39

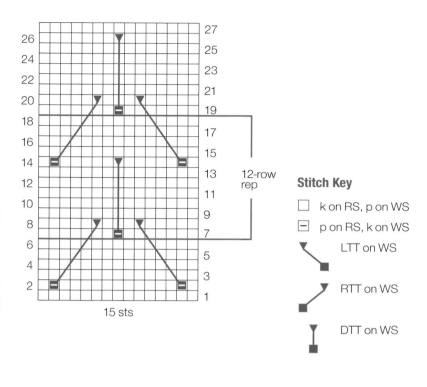

38

Upward Staghorn

(over 15 sts)

Rows 1, 3, and 5 (RS) Knit.

Row 2 P1, k1, p11, k1, p1.

Rows 4 and 6 Purl.

Row 7 K7, p1, k7.

Row 8 P5, RTT, p3, LTT, p5.

Rows 9, 11, and 13 Knit.

Rows 10 and 12 Purl.

Row 14 P1, k1, p5, DTT, p5, k1, p1.

Rows 15 and 17 Knit.

Rows 16 and 18 Purl.

Rep rows 7–18 as many times as necessary.

Rows 19–25 Rep rows 7–13.

Row 26 P7, DTT, p7.

Row 27 Knit.

Stitch Key

☐ k on RS, p on WS

⊟ p on RS, k on WS

▼ LTT on WS

▼ RTT on WS

▼ DTT on WS

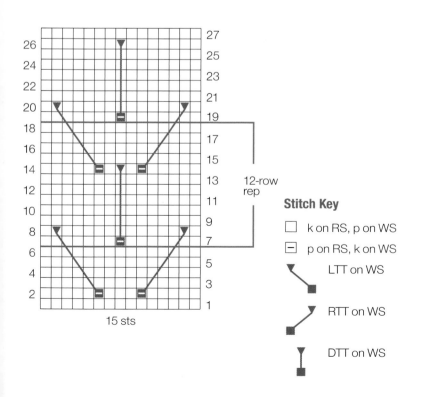

39

Downward Staghorn

(over 15 sts)

Rows 1, 3, and 5 (RS) Knit.

Row 2 P5, k1, p3, k1, p5.

Rows 4 and 6 Purl.

Row 7 K7, p1, k7.

Row 8 P1, LTT, p11, RTT, p1.

Rows 9, 11, and 13 Knit.

Rows 10 and 12 Purl.

Row 14 P5, k1, p1, DTT, p1, k1, p5.

Rows 15 and 17 Knit.

Rows 16 and 18 Purl.

Rep rows 7–18 as many times as necessary.

Rows 19–25 Rep rows 7–13.

Row 26 P7, DTT, p7.

Row 27 Knit.

Stitch Key

☐ k on RS, p on WS

⊟ p on RS, k on WS

▼ LTT on WS

▼ RTT on WS

▼ DTT on WS

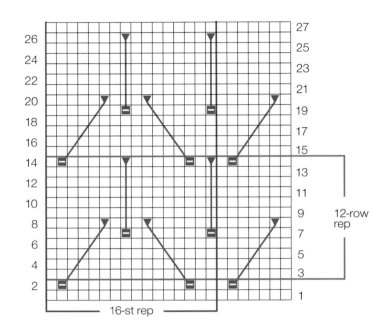

12-row rep

16-st rep

40

Staghorn Panel

(multiple of 16 sts plus 7 sts)

Row 1 (RS) Knit.

Row 2 *P1, k1, p11, k1, p2; rep from * to last 7 sts, p1, k1, p5.

Rows 3 and 5 Knit.

Rows 4 and 6 Purl.

Row 7 K7, *p1, k7, p1, k7; rep from * to end.

Row 8 *P5, RTT, p3, LTT, p6; rep from * to last 7 sts, p5, RTT, p1.

Rows 9, 11, and 13 Knit.

Rows 10 and 12 Purl.

Row 14 *P1, k1, p5, DTT, p5, k1, p1, DTT; rep from * to last 7 sts, p1, k1, p5.

Rep rows 3–14 as many times as necessary.

Rows 15–25 Rep rows 3–13.

Row 26 *P7, DTT, p7, DTT; rep from * to last 7 sts, p7.

Row 27 Knit.

Stitch Key

☐ k on RS, p on WS

⊟ p on RS, k on WS

 LTT on WS

RTT on WS

 DTT on WS

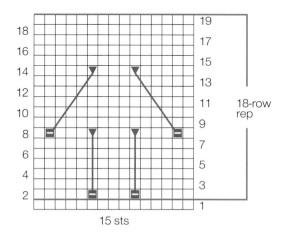

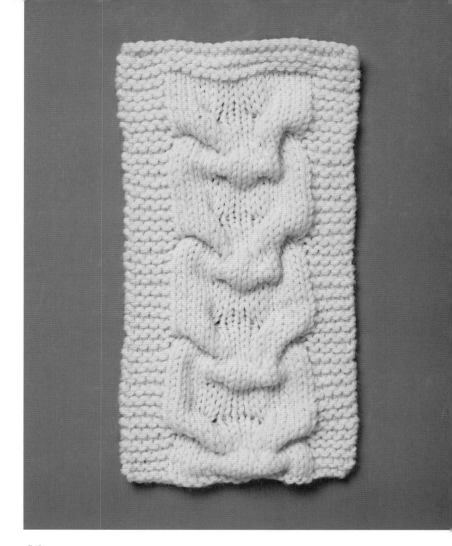

Stitch Key

☐ k on RS, p on WS

⊟ k on WS

 LTT on WS

 RTT on WS

 DTT on WS

41
Pearl Drops

(over 15 sts)

Row 1 and all RS rows Knit.

Row 2 P5, k1, p3, k1, p5.

Rows 4 and 6 Purl.

Row 8 P1, k1, p3, DTT, p3, DTT, p3, k1, p1.

Rows 10 and 12 Purl.

Row 14 P5, RTT, p3, LTT, p5.

Rows 16 and 18 Purl.

Row 19 Knit.

Rep rows 2–19.

42

43

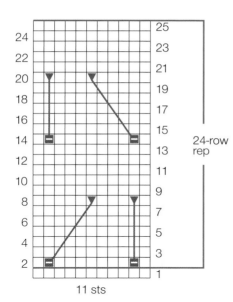

11 sts

24-row rep

42

Alternating Check Marks

(over 11 sts)

Row 1 and all RS rows Knit.

Row 2 P1, k1, p7, k1, p1.

Rows 4 and 6 Purl.

Row 8 P5, RTT, p3, DTT, p1.

Rows 10 and 12 Purl.

Row 14 P1, k1, p7, k1, p1.

Rows 16 and 18 Purl.

Row 20 P1, DTT, p3, LTT, p5.

Rows 22 and 24 Purl.

Row 25 Knit.

Rep rows 2–25.

Stitch Key

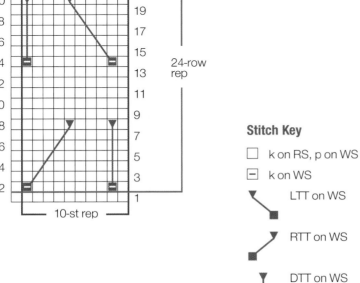

☐ k on RS, p on WS

⊟ k on WS

◥ LTT on WS

◢ RTT on WS

Y DTT on WS

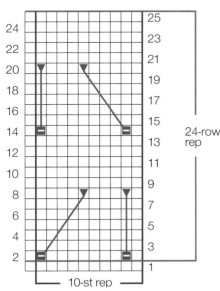

10-st rep

24-row rep

43

Alternating Check Marks Panel

(multiple of 10 sts plus 1 st)

Row 1 and all RS rows Knit.

Row 2 P1, *k1, p7, k1, p1; rep from * to end.

Rows 4 and 6 Purl.

Row 8 P1, *p4, RTT, p3, DTT, p1; rep from * to end.

Rows 10 and 12 Purl.

Row 14 P1, *k1, p7, k1, p1; rep from * to end.

Rows 16 and 18 Purl.

Row 20 P1, *DTT, p3, LTT, p5; rep from * to end.

Rows 22 and 24 Purl.

Row 25 Knit.

Rep rows 2–25.

Stitch Key

☐ k on RS, p on WS

⊟ k on WS

◥ LTT on WS

◢ RTT on WS

Y DTT on WS

ROPES, TWISTS, & WEAVES

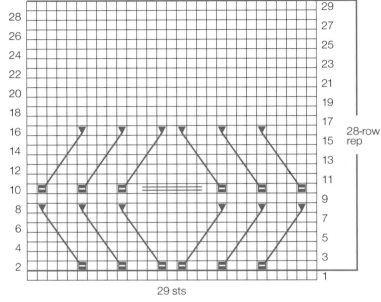

Stitch Key

☐ k on RS, p on WS

⊟ k on WS

▼ LTT on WS

▼ RTT on WS

⊞⊞⊞⊞ C7

44
Fancy Chain

(over 29 sts)

C7 (cinch 7) [Wyib sl 7 sts to RH needle, wyif sl 7 sts to LH needle] twice, pull yarn snug to cinch.

Row 1 and all RS rows Knit.

Row 2 P5, k1, p3, k1, p3, k1, p1, k1, p3, k1, p3, k1, p5.

Rows 4 and 6 Purl.

Row 8 P1, LTT, p3, LTT, p3, LTT, p9, RTT, p3, RTT, p3, RTT, p1.

Row 10 P1, k1, p3, k1, p3, k1, p1, C7, p7 (cinched sts), p1, k1, p3, k1, p3, k1, p1.

Rows 12 and 14 Purl.

Row 16 P5, RTT, p3, RTT, p3, RTT, p1, LTT, p3, LTT, p3, LTT, p5.

Rows 18, 20, 22, 24, 26, and 28 Purl.

Row 29 Knit.

Rep rows 2–29.

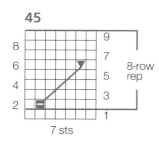

45

8-row rep

7 sts

Stitch Key

 k on RS, p on WS

 k on WS

LTT on WS

RTT on WS

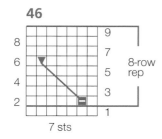

46

8-row rep

7 sts

45   46

45
Simple Left Twist
(over 7 sts)

46
Simple Right Twist
(over 7 sts)

Row 1 and all RS rows Knit.

Row 2 P1, k1, p5.

Row 4 Purl.

Row 6 P5, RTT, p1.

Row 8 Purl.

Row 9 Knit.

Rep rows 2–9.

Row 1 and all RS rows Knit.

Row 2 P5, k1, p1.

Row 4 Purl.

Row 6 P1, LTT, p5.

Row 8 Purl.

Row 9 Knit.

Rep rows 2–9.

ROPES, TWISTS, & WEAVES

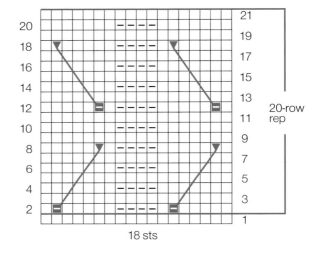

18 sts

20-row
rep

47
Double S-Rope

(over 18 sts)

Row 1 and all RS rows Knit.

Row 2 P1, k1, p5, k4, p1, k1, p5.

Rows 4 and 6 P7, k4, p7.

Row 8 P5, RTT, p1, k4, p5, RTT, p1.

Row 10 P7, k4, p7.

Row 12 P5, k1, p1, k4, p5, k1, p1.

Rows 14 and 16 P7, k4, p7.

Row 18 P1, LTT, p5, k4, p1, LTT, p5.

Row 20 P7, k4, p7.

Row 21 Knit.

Rep rows 2–21.

Stitch Key

☐ k on RS, p on WS

⊟ k on WS

◥ LTT on WS

◢ RTT on WS

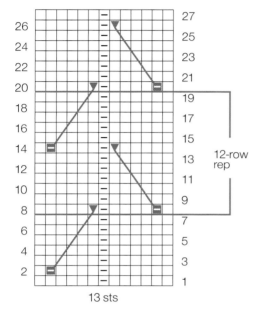

13 sts

Stitch Key

☐   k on RS, p on WS

⊟   p on RS, k on RS

▼   LTT on WS

◢   RTT on WS

48

Wavy Braid

(over 13 sts)

Row 1 and all RS rows K6, p1, k6.

Row 2 P1, k1, p4, k1, p6.

Rows 4 and 6 P6, k1, p6.

Row 8 P5, RTT, k1, p4, k1, p1.

Rows 10 and 12 P6, k1, p6.

Row 14 P1, k1, p4, k1, LTT, p5.

Rows 16 and 18 P6, k1, p6.

Row 19 K6, p1, k6.

Rep rows 8–19 as many times as necessary.

Rows 20–25 Rep rows 8–13.

Row 26 P6, k1, LTT, p5.

Row 27 K6, p1, k6.

49

50

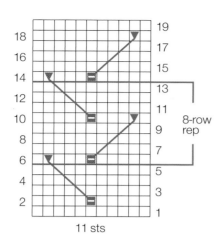

11 sts

8-row rep

Stitch Key

☐ k on RS, p on WS

⊟ k on WS

▼ LTT on WS

◢ RTT on WS

49

Basic Upward Braid

(over 11 sts)

Row 1 and all RS rows Knit.

Row 2 P5, k1, p5.

Row 4 Purl.

Row 6 P1, LTT, p3, k1, p5.

Row 8 Purl.

Row 10 P5, k1, p3, RTT, p1.

Row 12 Purl.

Row 13 Knit.

Rep rows 6–13 as many times as necessary.

Rows 14–17 Rep rows 6–9.

Row 18 P9, RTT, p1.

Row 19 Knit.

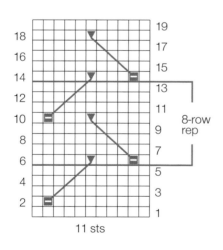

11 sts

8-row rep

Stitch Key

☐ k on RS, p on WS

⊟ k on WS

▼ LTT on WS

◢ RTT on WS

50

Basic Downward Braid

(over 11 sts)

Row 1 and all RS rows Knit.

Row 2 P1, k1, p9.

Row 4 Purl.

Row 6 P5, RTT, p3, k1, p1.

Row 8 Purl.

Row 10 P1, k1, p3, LTT, p5.

Row 12 Purl.

Row 13 Knit.

Rep rows 6–13 as many times as necessary.

Rows 14–17 Rep rows 6–9.

Row 18 P5, LTT, p5.

Row 19 Knit.

51

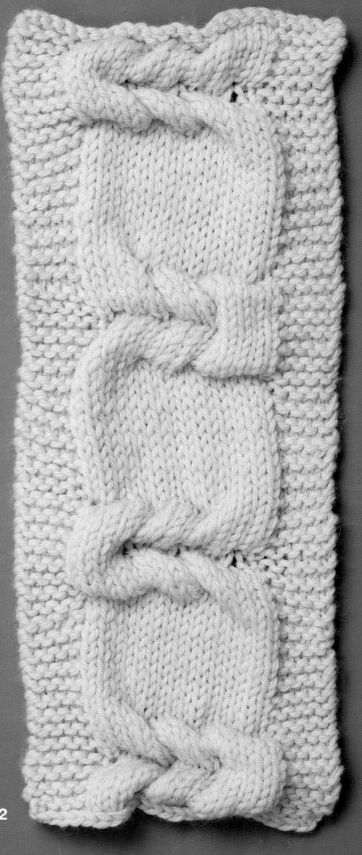

52

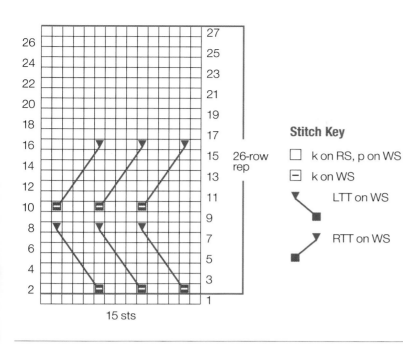

15 sts

26-row rep

Stitch Key

☐ k on RS, p on WS

⊟ k on WS

▼ LTT on WS

▼ RTT on WS

51

Horizontal Right Braided Chain

(over 15 sts)

Row 1 and all RS rows Knit.

Row 2 P5, k1, p3, k1, p3, k1, p1.

Rows 4 and 6 Purl.

Row 8 P1, LTT, p3, LTT, p3, LTT, p5.

Row 10 P1, k1, p3, k1, p3, k1, p5.

Rows 12 and 14 Purl.

Row 16 P5, RTT, p3, RTT, p3, RTT, p1.

Rows 18, 20, 22, 24, and 26 Purl.

Row 27 Knit.

Rep rows 2–27.

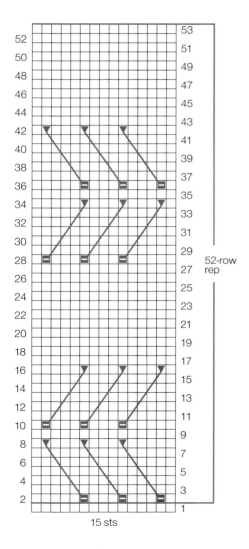

15 sts

52-row rep

Stitch Key

☐ k on RS, p on WS

⊟ k on WS

▼ LTT on WS

▼ RTT on WS

52

Horizontal Alternating Braided Chain

(over 15 sts)

Row 1 and all RS rows Knit.

Row 2 P5, k1, p3, k1, p3, k1, p1.

Rows 4 and 6 Purl.

Row 8 P1, LTT, p3, LTT, p3, LTT, p5.

Row 10 P1, k1, p3, k1, p3, k1, p5.

Rows 12 and 14 Purl.

Row 16 P5, RTT, p3, RTT, p3, RTT, p1.

Rows 18, 20, 22, 24, and 26 Purl.

Row 28 P1, k1, p3, k1, p3, k1, p5.

Rows 30 and 32 Purl.

Row 34 P5, RTT, p3, RTT, p3, RTT, p1.

Row 36 P5, k1, p3, k1, p3, k1, p1.

Rows 38 and 40 Purl.

Row 42 P1, LTT, p3, LTT, p3, LTT, p5.

Rows 44, 46, 48, 50, and 52 Purl.

Row 53 Knit.

Rep rows 2–53.

ROPES, TWISTS, & WEAVES

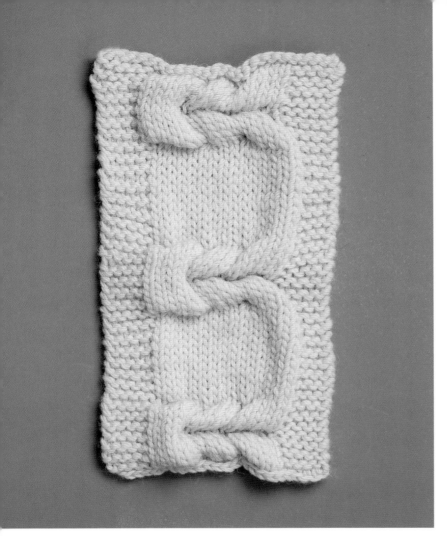

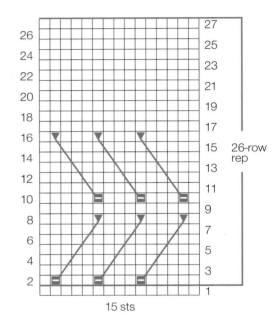

15 sts

26-row rep

53

Horizontal Left Braided Chain

(over 15 sts)

Row 1 and all RS rows Knit.

Row 2 P1, k1, p3, k1, p3, k1, p5.

Rows 4 and 6 Purl.

Row 8 P5, RTT, p3, RTT, p3, RTT, p1.

Row 10 P5, k1, p3, k1, p3, k1, p1.

Rows 12 and 14 Purl.

Row 16 P1, LTT, p3, LTT, p3, LTT, p5.

Rows 18, 20, 22, 24, and 26 Purl.

Row 27 Knit.

Rep rows 2–27.

Stitch Key

☐ k on RS, p on WS

⊟ k on WS

 LTT on WS

RTT on WS

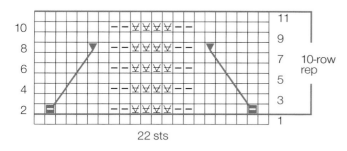

54

Center Rope with Twists

(over 22 sts)

Row 1 and all RS rows Knit.

Row 2 P1, k1, p5, k2, sl 4 wyif, k2, p5, k1, p1.

Rows 4 and 6 P7, k2, sl 4 wyif, k2, p7.

Row 8 P5, RTT, p1, k2, sl 4 wyif, k2, p1, LTT, p5.

Row 10 P7, k2, sl 4 wyif, k2, p7.

Row 11 Knit.

Rep rows 2–11.

Stitch Key

☐   k on RS, p on WS

⊟   k on WS

☒   sl 1 wyif

▼   LTT on WS

▼   RTT on WS

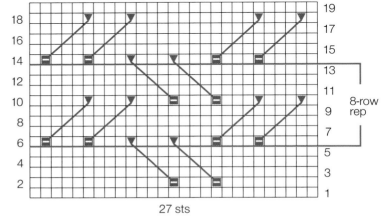

55

Ripples

(over 27 sts)

Row 1 and all RS rows Knit.

Row 2 P13, k1, p3, k1, p9.

Row 4 Purl.

Row 6 P1, k1, p3, k1, p3, LTT, p3, LTT, p3, k1, p3, k1, p5.

Row 8 Purl.

Row 10 P5, RTT, p3, RTT, p3, k1, p3, k1, p3, RTT, p3, RTT, p1.

Row 12 Purl.

Row 13 Knit.

Rep rows 6–13 as many times as necessary.

Rows 14–17 Rep rows 6–9.

Row 18 P5, RTT, p3, RTT, p11, RTT, p3, RTT, p1.

Row 19 Knit.

Stitch Key

☐ k on RS, p on WS

⊟ k on WS

▼ LTT on WS

▼ RTT on WS

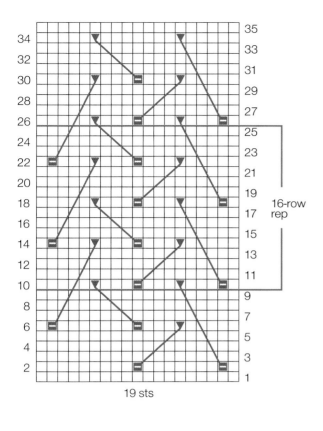

19 sts

56
Wide Weave

(over 19 sts)

Stitch Key

☐ k on RS, p on WS

⊟ k on WS

▼ LTT on WS

▼ RTT on WS

Row 1 and all RS rows Knit.

Row 2 P9, k1, p7, k1, p1.

Row 4 Purl.

Row 6 P1, k1, p7, k1, p3, RTT, p5.

Row 8 Purl.

Row 10 P5, LTT, p3, k1, p3, LTT, p3, k1, p1.

Row 12 Purl.

Row 14 P1, k1, p3, RTT, p3, k1, p3, RTT, p5.

Row 16 Purl.

Row 18 P5, LTT, p3, k1, p3, LTT, p3, k1, p1.

Row 20 Purl.

Row 22 P1, k1, p3, RTT, p3, k1, p3, RTT, p5.

Row 24 Purl.

Row 25 Knit.

Rep rows 10–25 as many times as necessary.

Row 26 P5, LTT, p3, k1, p3, LTT, p3, k1, p1.

Row 28 Purl.

Row 30 P5, RTT, p3, k1, p3, RTT, p5.

Row 32 Purl.

Row 34 P5, LTT, p7, LTT, p5.

Row 35 Knit.

57

58

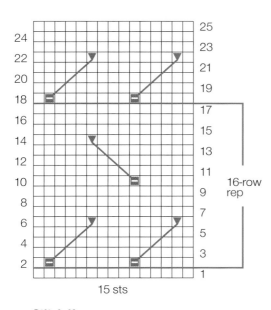

16-row rep

15 sts

Stitch Key

□ k on RS, p on WS

▬ k on WS

▼ LTT on WS

▼ RTT on WS

57

Plaited

(over 15 sts)

Row 1 and all RS rows Knit.

Row 2 P1, k1, p7, k1, p5.

Row 4 Purl.

Row 6 P5, RTT, p7, RTT, p1.

Row 8 Purl.

Row 10 P9, k1, p5.

Row 12 Purl.

Row 14 P5, LTT, p9.

Row 16 Purl.

Row 17 Knit.

Rep rows 2–17 as many times as necessary.

Rows 18–24 Rep rows 2–8.

Row 25 Knit.

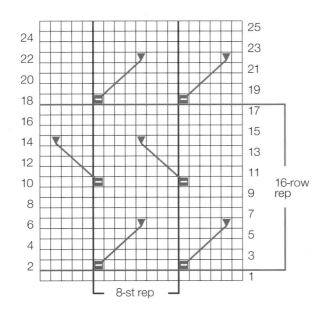

16-row rep

8-st rep

Stitch Key

□ k on RS, p on WS

▬ k on WS

▼ LTT on WS

▼ RTT on WS

58

Plaited Panel

(multiple of 8 sts plus 11 sts)

Row 1 and all RS rows Knit.

Row 2 P5, *k1, p7; rep from * to last 6 sts, k1, p5.

Row 4 Purl.

Row 6 P5, *p4, RTT, p3; rep from * to last 6 sts, p4, RTT, p1.

Row 8 Purl.

Row 10 P5, *k1, p7; rep from * to last 6 sts, k1, p5.

Row 12 Purl.

Row 14 P1, LTT, p3, *p4, LTT, p3; rep from * to last 6 sts, p6.

Row 16 Purl.

Row 17 Knit.

Rep rows 2–17 as many times as necessary.

Rows 18–24 Rep rows 2–8.

Row 25 Knit.

59

60

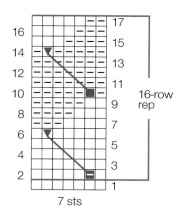

7 sts

16-row rep

59

Simple Right Twist with Alternating Stitches

(over 7 sts)

Note The Tuck Stitch on WS row 10 is a purl stitch in a row of knit stitches.

Rows 1, 3, and 5 (RS) Knit.

Row 2 P5, k1, p1.

Row 4 Purl.

Row 6 P1, LTT, p5.

Rows 7 and 8 K4, p3.

Row 9 K2, p5.

Row 10 K5, p1, k1.

Rows 11 and 13 Purl.

Row 12 Knit.

Row 14 K1, LTT, k5.

Rows 15 and 16 P4, k3.

Row 17 P2, k5.

Rep rows 2–17.

Stitch Key

☐ k on RS, p on WS

⊟ p on RS, k on WS

 LTT on WS

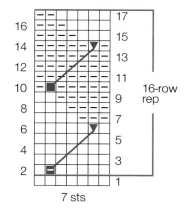

7 sts

16-row rep

60

Simple Left Twist with Alternating Stitches

(over 7 sts)

Note The Tuck Stitch on WS row 10 is a purl stitch in a row of knit stitches.

Rows 1, 3, and 5 (RS) Knit.

Row 2 P1, k1, p5.

Row 4 Purl.

Row 6 P5, RTT, p1.

Rows 7 and 8 P3, k4.

Row 9 P5, k2.

Row 10 K1, p1, k5.

Rows 11 and 13 Purl.

Row 12 Knit.

Row 14 K5, RTT, k1.

Rows 15 and 16 K3, p4.

Row 17 K5, p2.

Rep rows 2–17.

Stitch Key

☐ k on RS, p on WS

⊟ p on RS, k on WS

 RTT on WS

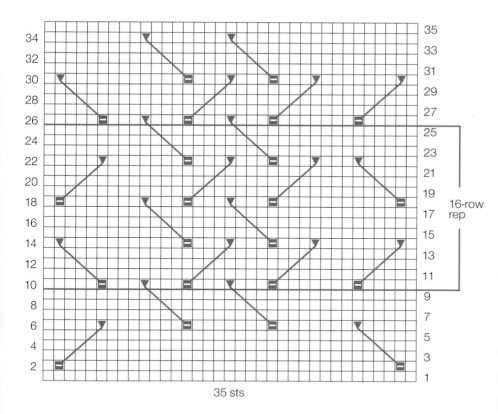

35 sts

Stitch Key

☐ k on RS, p on WS

⊟ k on WS

 LTT on WS

 RTT on WS

61
Center Weave with S-Ropes
(over 35 sts)

Row 1 and all RS rows Knit.

Row 2 P1, k1, p31, k1, p1.

Row 4 Purl.

Row 6 P5, RTT, p7, k1, p7, k1, p7, LTT, p5.

Row 8 Purl.

Row 10 P5, k1, p3, LTT, p3, k1, p3, LTT, p3, k1, p7, k1, p5.

Row 12 Purl.

Row 14 P1, LTT, p11, k1, p3, RTT, p3, k1, p3, RTT, p7, RTT, p1.

Row 16 Purl.

Row 18 P1, k1, p7, LTT, p3, k1, p3, LTT, p3, k1, p11, k1, p1.

Row 20 Purl.

Row 22 P5, RTT, p7, k1, p3, RTT, p3, k1, p3, RTT, p3, LTT, p5.

Row 24 Purl.

Row 25 Knit.

Rep rows 10–25 as many times as necessary.

Rows 26–33 Rep rows 10–17.

Row 34 P9, LTT, p7, LTT, p17.

Row 35 Knit.

62

63

64

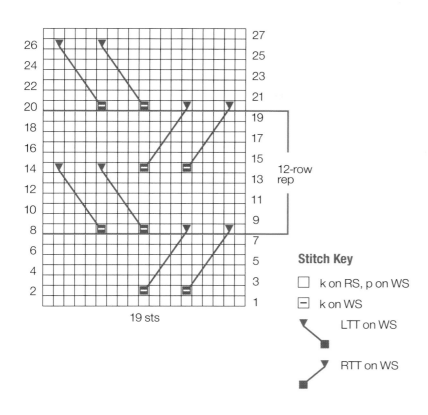

62
Upward Tweed

(over 19 sts)

Row 1 and all RS rows Knit.

Row 2 P9, k1, p3, k1, p5.

Rows 4 and 6 Purl.

Row 8 P5, k1, p3, k1, p3, RTT, p3, RTT, p1.

Rows 10 and 12 Purl.

Row 14 P1, LTT, p3, LTT, p3, k1, p3, k1, p5.

Rows 16 and 18 Purl.

Row 19 Knit.

Rep rows 8–19 as many times as necessary.

Rows 20–25 Rep rows 8–13.

Row 26 P1, LTT, p3, LTT, p13.

Row 27 Knit.

Stitch Key

☐ k on RS, p on WS

⊟ k on WS

▼ LTT on WS

▼ RTT on WS

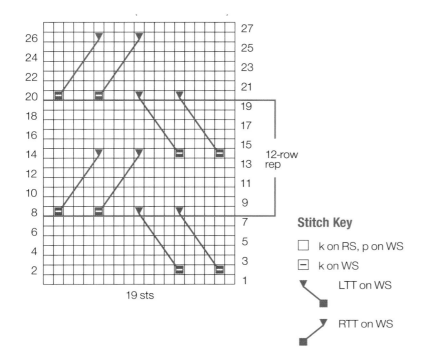

63
Downward Tweed

(over 19 sts)

Row 1 and all RS rows Knit.

Row 2 P13, k1, p3, k1, p1.

Rows 4 and 6 Purl.

Row 8 P1, k1, p3, k1, p3, LTT, p3, LTT, p5.

Rows 10 and 12 Purl.

Row 14 P5, RTT, p3, RTT, p3, k1, p3, k1, p1.

Rows 16 and 18 Purl.

Row 19 Knit.

Rep rows 8–19 as many times as necessary.

Rows 20–25 Rep rows 8–13.

Row 26 P5, RTT, p3, RTT, p9.

Row 27 Knit.

Stitch Key

☐ k on RS, p on WS

⊟ k on WS

▼ LTT on WS

▼ RTT on WS

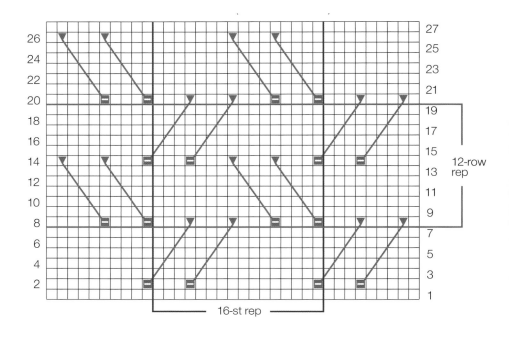

64

Tweed Panel

(multiple of 16 sts plus 19 sts)

Row 1 and all RS rows Knit.

Row 2 P9, k1, *p3, k1, p11, k1;
rep from * to last 9 sts, p3, k1, p5.

Rows 4 and 6 Purl.

Row 8 P5, k1, p3, k1, *p3, RTT,
p3, RTT, p3, k1, p3, k1; rep from *
to last 9 sts, p3, RTT, p3, RTT, p1.

Rows 10 and 12 Purl.

Row 14 P1, LTT, p3, LTT, p3, k1,
*p3, k1, p3, LTT, p3, LTT, p3, k1;
rep from * to last 9 sts, p3, k1, p5.

Rows 16 and 18 Purl.

Row 19 Knit.

Rep rows 8–19 as many times as
necessary.

Rows 20–25 Rep rows 8–13.

Row 26 P1, LTT, p3, LTT, p4, *p7,
LTT, p3, LTT, p4; rep from * to last 9
sts, p9.

Row 27 Knit.

Stitch Key

☐ k on RS, p on WS

⊟ k on WS

▼■ LTT on WS

▼■ RTT on WS

65

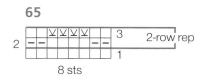

8 sts

Stitch Key

☐ k on RS, p on WS

⊟ k on WS ▼ LTT on WS

⦿ MSB

☑ sl 1 wyib RTT on WS

66

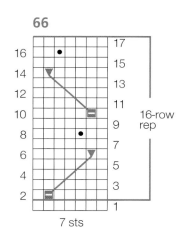

7 sts

16-row rep

65
Rope

(over 8 sts)

Row 1 (RS) Knit.

Row 2 K2, p4, k2.

Row 3 K2, sl 4 wyib, k2.

Rep rows 2 and 3.

66
Wave with Bobbles

(over 7 sts)

MSB (make small bobble) [K1, p1, k1, p1] in same st, [sl 4 sts from RH needle to LH needle as foll: (sl 1 wyib, sl 1 wyif) twice; k4] twice, pass 2nd, 3rd, and 4th sts over first st on RH needle.

Row 1 and all RS rows Knit.

Row 2 P1, k1, p5.

Row 4 Purl.

Row 6 P5, RTT, p1.

Row 8 P4, MSB, p2.

Row 10 P5, k1, p1.

Row 12 Purl.

Row 14 P1, LTT, p5.

Row 16 P2, MSB, p4.

Row 17 Knit.

Rep rows 2–17.

HYBRIDS

67

68

67

Bowties and Tietacks

(over 13 sts)

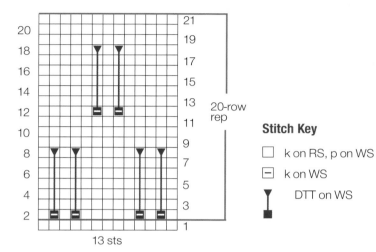

Stitch Key

☐ k on RS, p on WS

⊟ k on WS

▼ DTT on WS

Row 1 and all RS rows Knit.

Row 2 P1, k1, p1, k1, p5, k1, p1, k1, p1.

Rows 4 and 6 Purl.

Row 8 P1, DTT, p1, DTT, p5, DTT, p1, DTT, p1.

Row 10 Purl.

Row 12 P5, k1, p1, k1, p5.

Rows 14 and 16 Purl.

Row 18 P5, DTT, p1, DTT, p5.

Row 20 Purl.

Row 21 Knit.

Rep rows 2–21.

68

Bowties and Tietacks Panel

(multiple of 8 sts plus 5 sts)

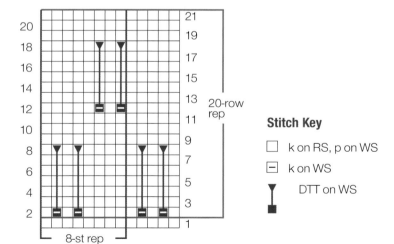

Stitch Key

☐ k on RS, p on WS

⊟ k on WS

▼ DTT on WS

Row 1 and all RS rows Knit.

Row 2 *P1, k1, p1, k1, p4; rep from * to last 5 sts, p1, k1, p1, k1, p1.

Rows 4 and 6 Purl.

Row 8 *P1, DTT, p1, DTT, p4; rep from * to last 5 sts, p1, DTT, p1, DTT, p1.

Row 10 Purl.

Row 12 *P5, k1, p1, k1; rep from * to last 5 sts, p5.

Rows 14 and 16 Purl.

Row 18 *P5, DTT, p1, DTT; rep from * to last 5 sts, p5.

Row 20 Purl.

Row 21 Knit.

Rep rows 2–21.

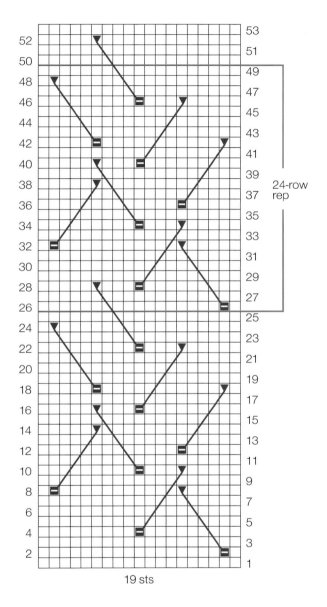

19 sts

Stitch Key

☐ k on RS, p on WS

⊟ k on WS

 LTT on WS

RTT on WS

69

Leaves and Thorns

(over 19 sts)

Row 1 and all RS rows Knit.

Row 2 P17, k1, p1.

Row 4 P9, k1, p9.

Row 6 Purl.

Row 8 P1, k1, p11, LTT, p5.

Row 10 P9, k1, p3, RTT, p5.

Row 12 P13, k1, p5.

Row 14 P5, RTT, p13.

Row 16 P5, LTT, p3, k1, p9.

Row 18 P5, k1, p11, RTT, p1.

Row 20 Purl.

Row 22 P9, k1, p3, RTT, p5.

Row 24 P1, LTT, p17.

Row 26 P17, k1, p1.

Row 28 P5, LTT, p3, k1, p9.

Row 30 Purl.

Row 32 P1, k1, p11, LTT, p5.

Row 34 P9, k1, p3, RTT, p5.

Row 36 P13, k1, p5.

Row 38 P5, RTT, p13.

Row 40 P5, LTT, p3, k1, p9.

Row 42 P5, k1, p11, RTT, p1.

Row 44 Purl.

Row 46 P9, k1, p3, RTT, p5.

Row 48 P1, LTT, p17.

Row 49 Knit.

Rep rows 26–49 as many times as necessary.

Row 50 Purl.

Row 52 P5, LTT, p13.

Row 53 Knit.

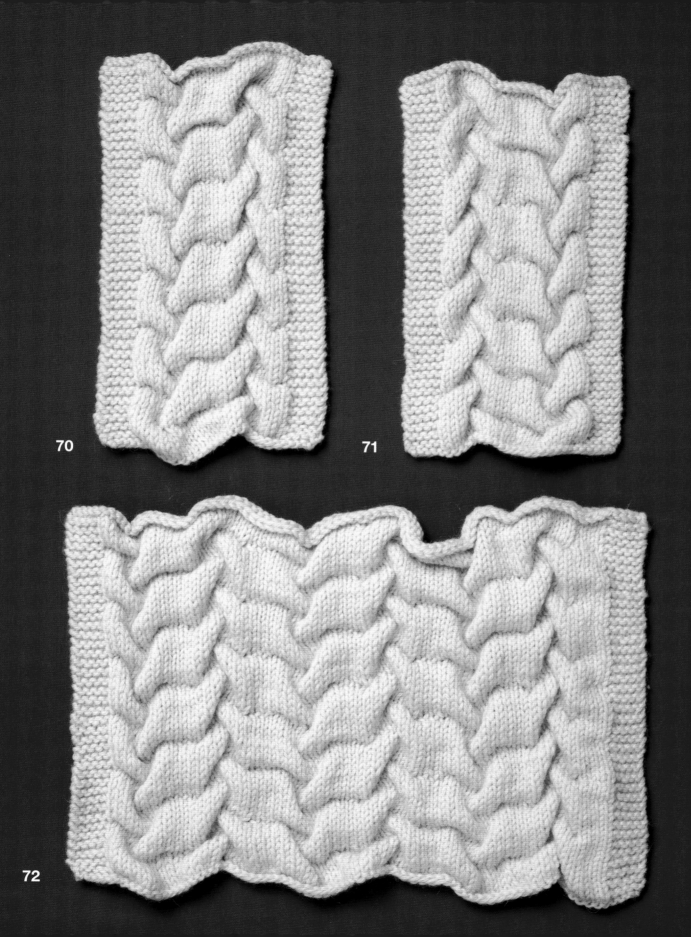

70

71

72

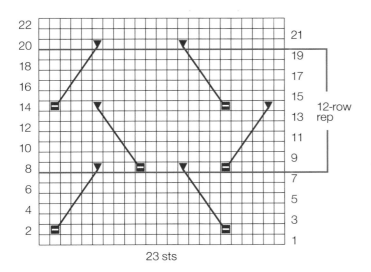

70
Right Rhombus

(over 23 sts)

Row 1 and all RS rows Knit.

Row 2 P1, k1, p15, k1, p5.

Rows 4 and 6 Purl.

Row 8 P5, RTT, p3, k1, p3, LTT, p3, k1, p5.

Rows 10 and 12 Purl.

Row 14 P1, k1, p3, LTT, p11, k1, p3, RTT, p1.

Rows 16 and 18 Purl.

Row 19 Knit.

Rep rows 8–19 as many times as necessary.

Row 20 P5, RTT, p7, LTT, p9.

Row 22 Purl.

23 sts

Stitch Key

☐ k on RS, p on WS

⊟ k on WS

 LTT on WS

RTT on WS

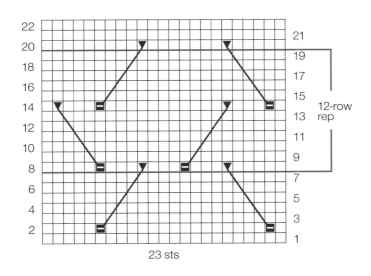

71
Left Rhombus

(over 23 sts)

Row 1 and all RS rows Knit.

Row 2 P5, k1, p15, k1, p1.

Rows 4 and 6 Purl.

Row 8 P5, k1, p3, RTT, p3, k1, p3, LTT, p5.

Rows 10 and 12 Purl.

Row 14 P1, LTT, p3, k1, p11, RTT, p3, k1, p1.

Rows 16 and 18 Purl.

Row 19 Knit.

Rep rows 8–19 as many times as necessary.

Row 20 P9, RTT, p7, LTT, p5.

Row 22 Purl.

23 sts

Stitch Key

☐ k on RS, p on WS

⊟ k on WS

 LTT on WS

RTT on WS

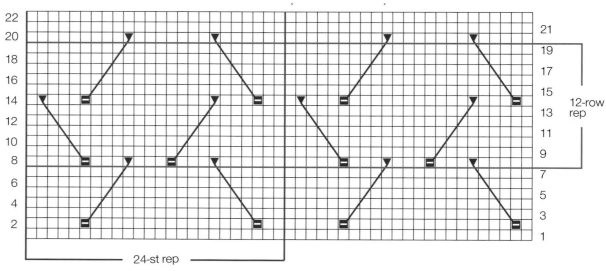

24-st rep

12-row rep

72

Rhombus Panel

(multiple of 24 sts plus 23 sts)

Row 1 and all RS rows Knit.

Row 2 *P5, k1, p15, k1, p2; rep from *

to last 23 sts, p5, k1, p15, k1, p1.

Rows 4 and 6 Purl.

Row 8 *P5, k1, p3, RTT, p3, k1, p3,

LTT, p6; rep from * to last 23 sts, p5, k1,

p3, RTT, p3, k1, p3, LTT, p5.

Rows 10 and 12 Purl.

Row 14 *P1, LTT, p3, k1, p11, RTT, p3,

k1, p2; rep from * to last 23 sts, p1, LTT,

p3, k1, p11, RTT, p3, k1, p1.

Rows 16 and 18 Purl.

Row 19 Knit.

Rep rows 8–19 as many times as

necessary.

Row 20 *P9, RTT, p7, LTT, p6; rep from

* to last 23 sts, P9, RTT, p7, LTT, p5.

Row 22 Purl.

Stitch Key

☐ k on RS, p on WS

⊟ k on WS

↘■ LTT on WS

↘■ RTT on WS

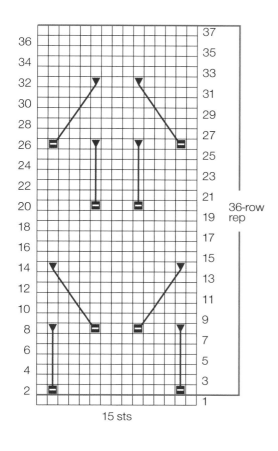

36-row rep

15 sts

Stitch Key

☐ k on RS, p on WS

⊟ k on WS

 LTT on WS

 RTT on WS

 DTT on WS

73

Half Hitch

(over 15 sts)

Row 1 and all RS rows Knit.

Row 2 P1, k1, p11, k1, p1.

Rows 4 and 6 Purl.

Row 8 P1, DTT, p3, k1, p3, k1, p3, DTT, p1.

Rows 10 and 12 Purl.

Row 14 P1, LTT, p11, RTT, p1.

Rows 16 and 18 Purl.

Row 20 P5, k1, p3, k1, p5.

Rows 22 and 24 Purl.

Row 26 P1, k1, p3, DTT, p3, DTT, p3, k1, p1.

Rows 28 and 30 Purl.

Row 32 P5, RTT, p3, LTT, p5.

Rows 34 and 36 Purl.

Row 37 Knit.

Rep rows 2–37.

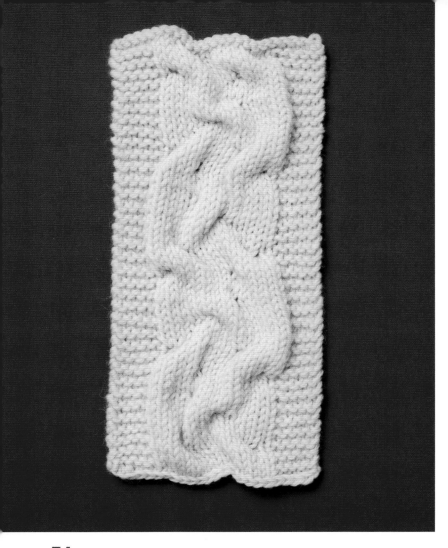

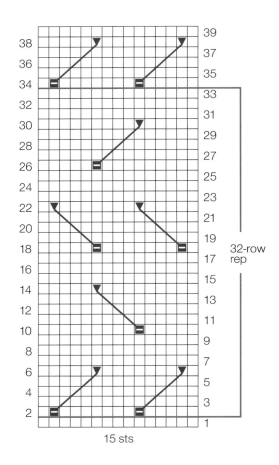

15 sts

32-row rep

74

Meandering

(over 15 sts)

Row 1 and all RS rows Knit.

Row 2 P1, k1, p7, k1, p5.

Row 4 Purl.

Row 6 P5, RTT, p7, RTT, p1.

Row 8 Purl.

Row 10 P9, k1, p5.

Row 12 Purl.

Row 14 P5, LTT, p9.

Row 16 Purl.

Row 18 P5, k1, p7, k1, p1.

Row 20 Purl.

Row 22 P1, LTT, p7, LTT, p5.

Row 24 Purl.

Row 26 P5, k1, p9.

Row 28 Purl.

Row 30 P9, RTT, p5.

Row 32 Purl.

Row 33 Knit.

Rep rows 2–33 as any times as

necessary.

Rows 34–38 Rep rows 2–6.

Row 39 Knit.

Stitch Key

☐ k on RS, p on WS

⊟ k on WS

 LTT on WS

RTT on WS

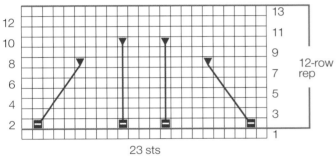

23 sts

Stitch Key

 k on RS, p on WS

k on WS

 LTT on WS

 RTT on WS

 DTT on WS

75
Checks and Dots

(over 23 sts)

Row 1 and all RS rows Knit.

Row 2 P1, k1, p7, k1, p3, k1, p7, k1, p1.

Rows 4 and 6 Purl.

Row 8 P5, RTT, p11, LTT, p5.

Row 10 P9, DTT, p3, DTT, p9.

Row 12 Purl.

Row 13 Knit.

Rep rows 2–13.

HYBRIDS

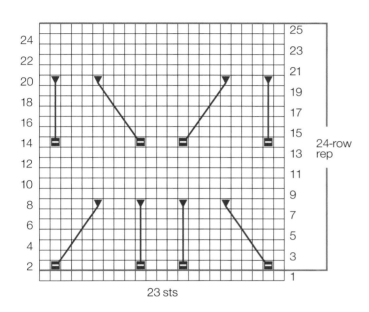

23 sts

Stitch Key

	k on RS, p on WS
	k on WS

 LTT on WS

 RTT on WS

 DTT on WS

76

Mirrored Double-Wide

(over 23 sts)

Row 1 and all RS rows Knit.

Row 2 P1, k1, p7, k1, p3, k1, p7, k1, p1.

Rows 4 and 6 Purl.

Row 8 P5, RTT, p3, DTT, p3, DTT, p3, LTT, p5.

Rows 10 and 12 Purl.

Row 14 P1, k1, p7, k1, p3, k1, p7, k1, p1.

Rows 16 and 18 Purl.

Row 20 P1, DTT, p3, LTT, p11, RTT, p3, DTT, p1.

Rows 22 and 24 Purl.

Row 25 Knit.

Rep rows 2–25.

HYBRIDS

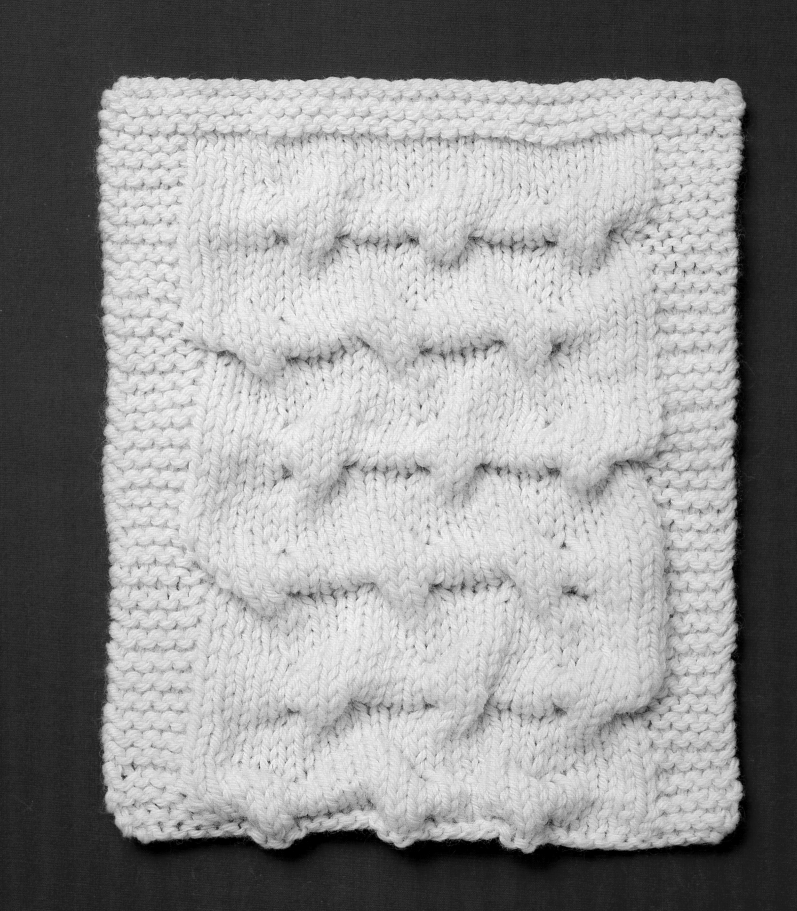

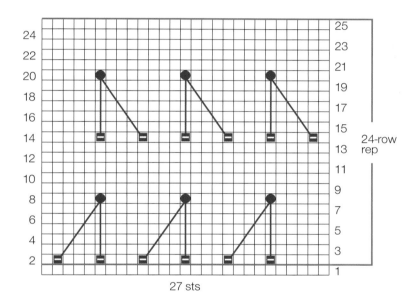

24-row rep

27 sts

Stitch Key

☐ k on RS, p on WS

⊟ k on WS

 DRTT on WS

 LDTT on WS

77
Barbed Wire

(over 27 sts)

Row 1 and all RS rows Knit.

Row 2 P1, k1, p3, k1, p3, k1, p3, k1, p3, k1, p3, k1, p5.

Rows 4 and 6 Purl.

Row 8 P5, DRTT, p7, DRTT, p7, DRTT, p5.

Rows 10 and 12 Purl.

Row 14 P5, k1, p3, k1, p3, k1, p3, k1, p3, k1, p3, k1, p1.

Rows 16 and 18 Purl.

Row 20 P5, LDTT, p7, LDTT, p7, LDTT, p5.

Rows 22 and 24 Purl.

Row 25 Knit.

Rep rows 2–25.

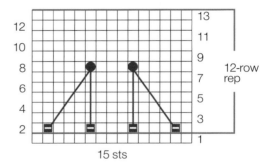

13
12
11
10
9
8
7
6
5
4
3
2
1

12-row rep

15 sts

78

Fangs

(over 15 sts)

Row 1 and all RS rows Knit.

Row 2 P1, k1, p3, k1, p3, k1, p3, k1, p1.

Rows 4 and 6 Purl.

Row 8 P5, DRTT, p3, LDTT, p5.

Rows 10 and 12 Purl.

Row 13 Knit.

Rep rows 2–13.

Stitch Key

☐ k on RS, p on WS

⊟ k on WS

 DRTT on WS

 LDTT on WS

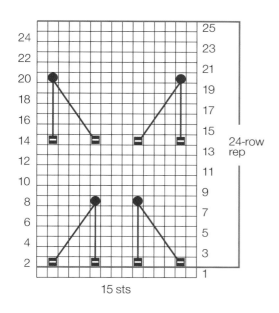

15 sts

Stitch Key

☐ k on RS, p on WS

⊟ k on WS

 DRTT on WS

 LDTT on WS

79

Hinges

(over 15 sts)

Row 1 and all RS rows Knit.

Row 2 P1, k1, p3, k1, p3, k1, p3, k1, p1.

Rows 4 and 6 Purl.

Row 8 P5, DRTT, p3, LDTT, p5.

Rows 10 and 12 Purl.

Row 14 P1, k1, p3, k1, p3, k1, p3, k1, p1.

Rows 16 and 18 Knit.

Row 20 P1, LDTT, p11, DRTT, p1.

Rows 22 and 24 Purl.

Row 25 Knit.

Rep rows 2–25.

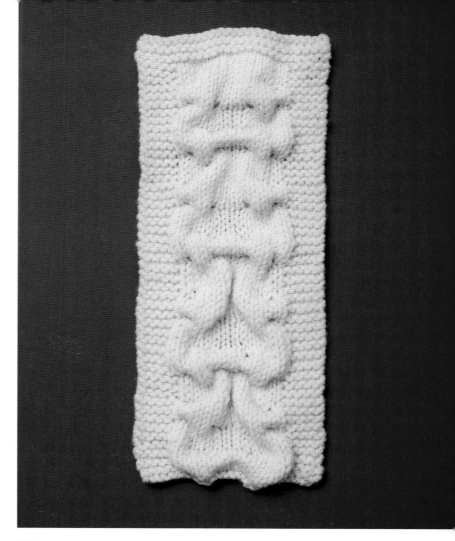

ALLOVER & HORIZONTAL BANDS

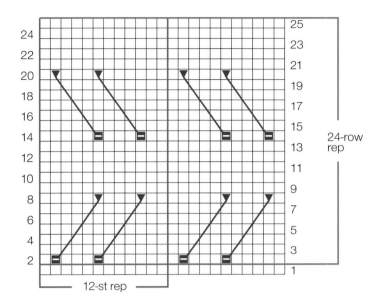

24-row rep

12-st rep

Stitch Key

☐ k on RS, p on WS

⊟ k on WS

▼ LTT on WS

▼ RTT on WS

80

Interlocking Links

(multiple of 12 sts plus 11 sts)

Row 1 and all RS rows Knit.

Row 2 *P1, k1, p3, k1, p6; rep from * to last 11 sts, p1, k1, p3, k1, p5.

Rows 4 and 6 Purl.

Row 8 *P5, RTT, p3, RTT, p2; rep from * to last 11 sts, p5, RTT, p3, RTT, p1.

Rows 10 and 12 Purl.

Row 14 *P5, k1, p3, k1, p2; rep from * to last 11 sts, p5, k1, p3, k1, p1.

Rows 16 and 18 Purl.

Row 20 *P1, LTT, p3, LTT, p6; rep from * to last 11 sts, k1, LTT, p3, LTT, p5.

Rows 22 and 24 Purl.

Row 25 Knit.

Rep rows 2–25.

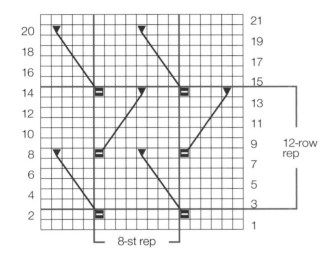

8-st rep

Stitch Key

☐ k on RS, p on WS

⊟ k on WS

▼ LTT on WS

▼ RTT on WS

12-row rep

81
Tight Weave

(multiple of 8 sts plus 11 sts)

Row 1 and all RS rows Knit.

Row 2 P5, *k1, p7; rep from * to last 6 sts, k1, p5.

Rows 4 and 6 Purl.

Row 8 P1, LTT, p3, *k1, p3, LTT, p3; rep from * to last 6 sts, k1, p5.

Rows 10 and 12 Purl.

Row 14 P5, *k1, p3, RTT, p3; rep from * to last 6 sts, k1, p3, RTT, p1.

Rep rows 3–14 as many times as necessary.

Rows 15–19 Rep rows 3–7.

Row 20 P1, LTT, p3, *p4, LTT, p3; rep from * to last 6 sts, p6.

Row 21 Knit.

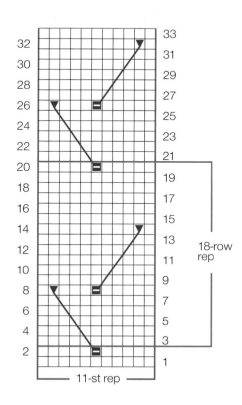

Stitch Key

☐ k on RS, p on WS

⊟ k on WS

▼ LTT on WS

▼ RTT on WS

82

Loose Weave

(multiple of 11 sts)

Row 1 and all RS rows Knit.

Row 2 *P5, k1, p5; rep from * to end.

Rows 4 and 6 Purl.

Row 8 *P1, LTT, p3, k1, p5; rep from * to end.

Rows 10 and 12 Purl.

Row 14 *P9, RTT, p1; rep from * to end.

Rows 16 and 18 Purl.

Row 20 *P5, k1, p5; rep from * to end.

Rep rows 3–20 as many times as necessary.

Rows 21–32 Rep rows 3–14.

Row 33 Knit.

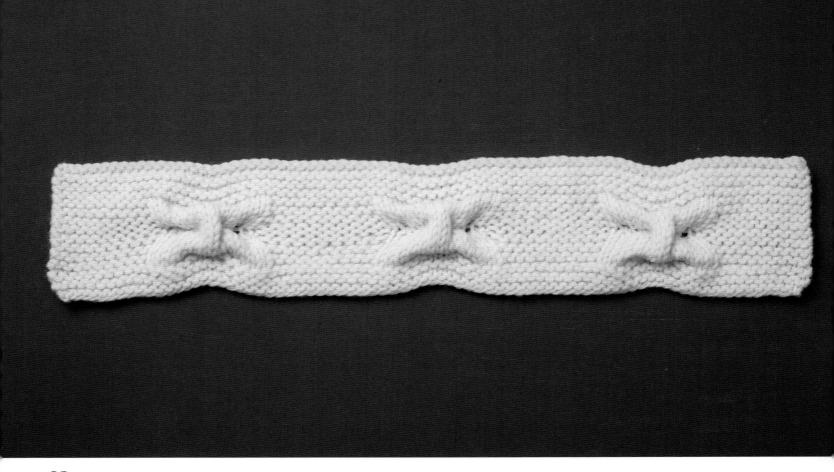

83

Horizontal X-box

(multiple of 23 sts plus 10 sts)

Row 1 and all RS rows Knit.

Row 2 *K10, p13; rep from * to last 10 sts, k10.

Row 4 *K10, p5, k1, p1, k1, p5; rep from * to last 10 sts, k10.

Rows 6 and 8 Rep row 2.

Row 10 *K10, p1, LTT, p9, RTT, p1; rep from * to last 10 sts, k10.

Row 12 *K10, p1, k1, p9, k1, p1; rep from * to last 10 sts, k10.

Rows 14 and 16 Rep row 2.

Row 18 *K10, p5, RTT, p1, LTT, p5; rep from * to last 10 sts, k10.

Row 20 Rep row 2.

Row 21 Knit.

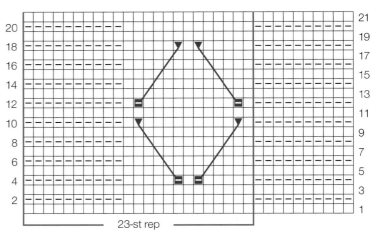

23-st rep

Stitch Key

☐ k on RS, p on WS

⊟ k on WS

  LTT on WS

  RTT on WS

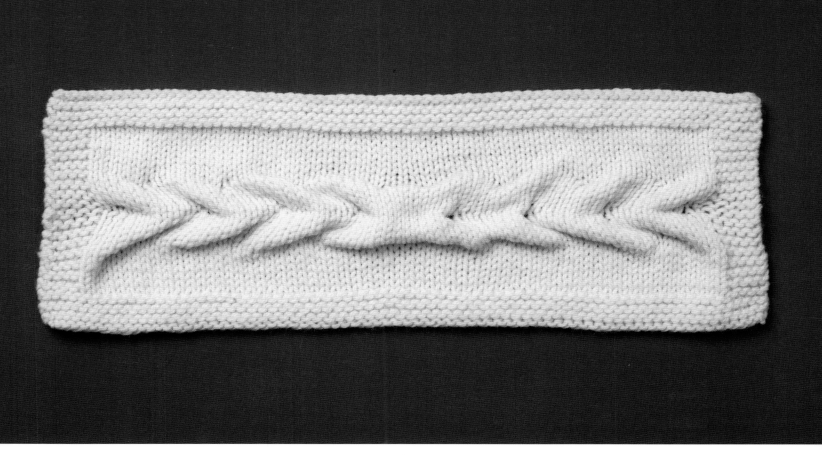

84

Horizontal X-box with Inward Arrows

(multiple of 16 sts plus 15 sts)

Row 1 and all RS rows Knit.

Row 2 Purl.

Row 4 *P5, k1, p2; rep from * as many times as necessary, p5, k1, p3 (center sts), k1, p5, **p2, k1, p5; rep from ** to end.

Rows 6 and 8 Purl.

Row 10 *P1, LTT, p6; rep from * as many times as necessary, p1, LTT, p4, p3 (center sts), p4, RTT, p1, **p6, RTT, p1; rep from ** to end.

Row 12 *P1, k1, p6; rep from * as many times as necessary, p1, k1, p4, p3 (center sts), p4, k1, p1, **p6, k1, p1; rep from ** to end.

Rows 14 and 16 Purl.

Row 18 *P5, RTT, p2; rep from * as many times as necessary, p5, RTT, p3 (center sts), LTT, p5, **p2, LTT, p5, rep from ** to end.

Row 20 Purl.

Row 21 Knit.

Stitch Key

 k on RS, p on WS

k on WS

 LTT on WS

RTT on WS

Center sts

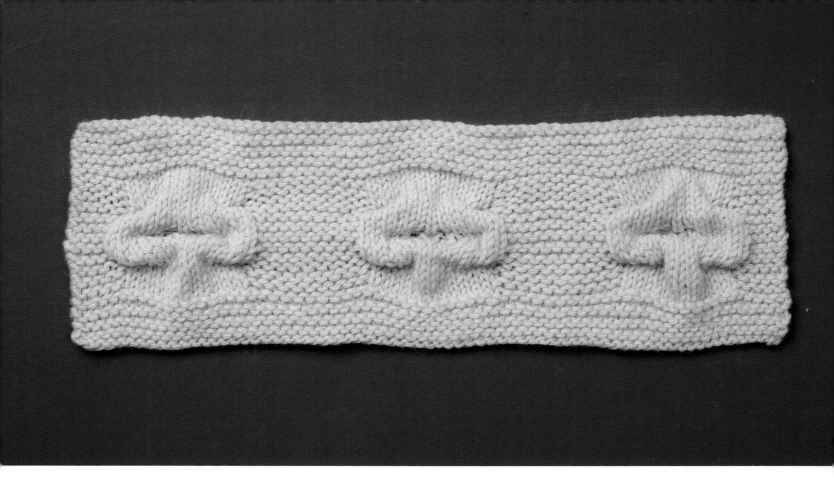

85

Horizontal Diamonds with Garter Spacing

(multiple of 23 sts plus 10 sts)

Row 1 and all RS rows Knit.

Rows 2 and 4 *K10, p13; rep from * to last 10 sts, k10.

Row 6 *K10, p1, k1, p9, k1, p1; rep from * to last 10 sts, k10.

Rows 8 and 10 Rep row 2.

Row 12 *K10, p5, RTT, p1, LTT, p5; rep from * to last 10 sts, k10.

Row 14 *K10, p5, k1, p1, k1, p5; rep from * to last 10 sts, k10.

Rows 16 and 18 Rep row 2.

Row 20 *K10, p1, LTT, p9, RTT, p1; rep from * to last 10 sts, k10.

Rows 22 and 24 *K10, p13; rep from * to last 10 sts, k10.

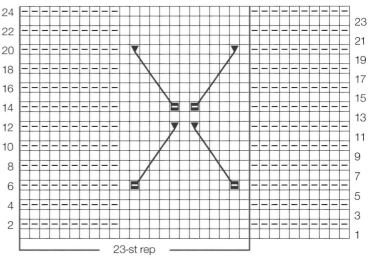

23-st rep

Stitch Key

☐ k on RS, p on WS

⊟ k on WS

 LTT on WS

RTT on WS

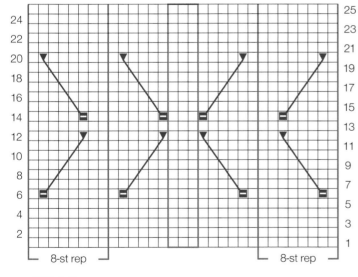

24															25
22															23
20															21
18															19
16															17
14															15
12															13
10															11
8															9
6															7
4															5
2															3
															1

└ 8-st rep ┘   └ 8-st rep ┘

Stitch Key

☐ k on RS, p on WS

⊟ k on WS

◣ LTT on WS

◥ RTT on WS

◼ RTT on WS (filled marker)

☐☐☐ Center sts

86

Center Diamond with Outward Arrows

(multiple of 16 sts plus 15 sts)

Row 1 and all RS rows Knit.

Rows 2 and 4 Purl.

Row 6 *P1, k1, p6; rep from * as many times as necessary, p1, k1, p4, p3 (center sts), p4, k1, p1, **p6, k1, p1; rep from ** to end.

Rows 8 and 10 Purl.

Row 12 *P5, RTT, p2; rep from * as many times as necessary, p5,

RTT, p3 (center sts), LTT, p5, **p2, LTT, p5; rep from ** to end.

Row 14 *P5, k1, p2; rep from * as many times as necessary, p5, k1, p3 (center sts), k1, p5, **p2, k1, p5; rep from ** to end.

Rows 16 and 18 Purl.

Row 20 *P1, LTT, p6; rep from * as many times as necessary, p1, LTT, p4, p3 (center sts), p4, RTT, p1, **p6, RTT, p1; rep from ** to end.

Rows 22 and 24 Purl.

Row 25 Knit.

125

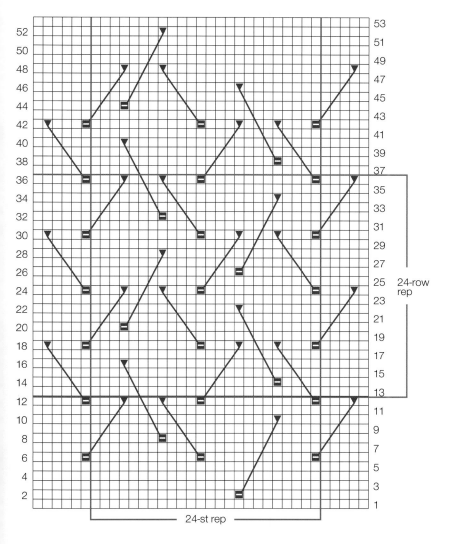

87
Avian Tracks

(multiple of 24 sts plus 11 sts)

Row 1 and all RS rows Knit.

Row 2 P6, *p15, k1, p8; rep from * to last 5 sts, p5.

Row 4 Purl.

Row 6 P5, k1, *p11, k1, p11, k1; rep from * to last 5 sts, p5.

Row 8 P6, *p7, k1, p16; rep from * to last 5 sts, p5.

Row 10 P6, *p19, RTT, p4; rep from * to last 5 sts, p5.

Row 12 P5, k1, *p3, RTT, p3, LTT, p3, k1, p11, k1; rep from * to last 5 sts, p3, RTT, p1.

Row 14 P6, *p19, k1, p4; rep from * to last 5 sts, p5.

Row 16 P6, *p3, LTT, p20; rep from * to last 5 sts, p5.

Row 18 P1, LTT, p3, k1, *p11, k1, p3, RTT, p3, LTT, p3, k1; rep from * to last 5 sts, p5.

Row 20 P6, *p3, k1, p20; rep from * to last 5 sts, p5.

Row 22 P6, *p15, LTT, p8; rep from * to last 5 sts, p5.

Row 24 P5, k1, *p3, RTT, p3, LTT, p3, k1, p11, k1; rep from * to last 5 sts, p3, RTT, p1.

Row 26 P6, *p15, k1, p8; rep from * to last 5 sts, p5.

Row 28 P6, *p7, RTT, p16; rep from * to last 5 sts, p5.

Row 30 P1, LTT, p3, k1, *p11, k1, p3, RTT, p3, LTT, p3, k1; rep from * to last 5 sts, p5.

Row 32 P6, *p7, k1, p16; rep from * to last 5 sts, p5.

Row 34 P6, *p19, RTT, p4; rep from * to last 5 sts, p5.

Row 36 P5, k1, *p3, RTT, p3, LTT, p3, k1, p11, k1; rep from * to last 5 sts, p3, RTT, p1.

Rep rows 13–36 as many times as necessary.

Rows 37–47 Rep rows 13–23.

Row 48 P6, *p3, RTT, p3, LTT, p16; rep from * to last 5 sts, p3, RTT, p1.

Row 50 Purl.

Row 52 P6, *p7, RTT, p16; rep from * to last 5 sts, p5.

Row 53 Knit.

Stitch Key

☐ k on RS, p on WS

⊟ k on WS

 LTT on WS

 RTT on WS

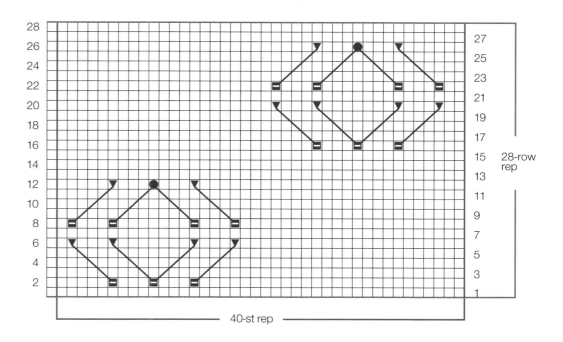

Stitch Key

☐ k on RS, p on WS

⊟ k on WS

▼ LTT on WS

▼ RTT on WS

▽ SL7RTT on WS

⩘ LRTT on WS

88

Ribbons and Bows

(multiple of 40 sts plus 1 st)

Row 1 and all RS rows Knit.

Row 2 P1, *p5, k1, p3, k1, p3, k1, p26; rep from * to end.

Row 4 Purl.

Row 6 P1, *p1, LTT, p3, SL7RTT, p3, RTT, p22; rep from * to end.

Row 8 P1, *p1, k1, p3, k1, p7, k1, p3, k1, p22; rep from * to end.

Row 10 Purl.

Row 12 P1, *p5, RTT, p3, LRTT, p3, LTT, p26; rep from * to end.

Row 14 Purl.

Row 16 P1, *p25, k1, p3, k1, p3, k1, p6; rep from * to end.

Row 18 Purl.

Row 20 P1, *p21, LTT, p3, SL7RTT, p3, RTT, p2; rep from * to end.

Row 22 P1, *p21, k1, p3, k1, p7, k1, p3, k1, p2; rep from * to end.

Row 24 Purl.

Row 26 P1, *p25, RTT, p3, LRTT, p3, LTT, p6; rep from * to end.

Row 28 Purl.

Rep rows 1–28.

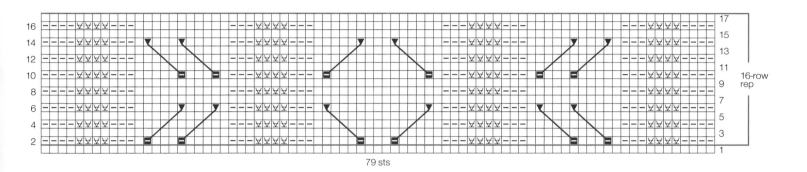

16-row rep

79 sts

Stitch Key

☐ k on RS, p on WS
⊟ k on WS
☒ sl 1 wyif
◥ LTT on WS
◢ RTT on WS

89
Cable Panel

(over 79 sts)

Row 1 and all RS rows Knit.

Row 2 K4, sl 4 wyif, k3, p1, k1, p3, k1, p5, k3, sl 4 wyif, k3, p5, k1, p3, k1, p5, k3, sl 4 wyif, k3, p5, k1, p3, k1, p1, k3, sl 4 wyif, k4.

Row 4 K4, sl 4 wyif, k3, p11, k3, sl 4 wyif, k3, p15, k3, sl 4 wyif, k3, p11, k3, sl 4 wyif, k4.

Row 6 K4, sl 4 wyif, k3, p5, RTT, p3, RTT, p1, k3, sl 4 wyif, k3, p1, LTT, p11, RTT, p1, k3, sl 4 wyif, k3, p1, LTT, p3, LTT, p5, k3, sl 4 wyif, k4.

Row 8 K4, sl 4 wyif, k3, p11, k3, sl 4 wyif, k3, p15, k3, sl 4 wyif, k3, p11, k3, sl 4 wyif, k4.

Row 10 K4, sl 4 wyif, k3, p5, k1, p3, k1, p1, k3, sl 4 wyif, k3, p1, k1, p11, k1, p1, k3, sl 4 wyif, k3, p1, k1, p3, k1, p5, k3, sl 4 wyif, k4.

Row 12 K4, sl 4 wyif, k3, p11, k3, sl 4 wyif, k3, p15, k3, sl 4 wyif, k3, p11, k3, sl 4 wyif, k4.

Row 14 K4, sl 4 wyif, k3, p1, LTT, p3, LTT, p5, k3, sl 4 wyif, k3, p5, RTT, p3, LTT, p5, k3, sl 4 wyif, k3, p5, RTT, p3, RTT, p1, k3, sl 4 wyif, k4.

Row 16 K4, sl 4 wyif, k3, p11, k3, sl 4 wyif, k3, p15, k3, sl 4 wyif, k3, p11, k3, sl 4 wyif, k4.

Row 17 Knit.

Rep rows 2–17.

131

THE PROJECTS

RHOMBULKY COWL

A soft and bulky alpaca/wool yarn is the perfect complement to any cowl, especially this strikingly structured rhomboid shape. Not only will it keep wintry chills at bay, it's an undeniable showstopper.

SKILL LEVEL
■■■□

KNITTED MEASUREMENTS

Circumference 35"/89cm

Width 13"/33cm

MATERIALS

- 4 3½oz/100g skeins (each approx 45yd/41m) of Blue Sky Fibers *Bulky* (alpaca/wool) in #1211 Frost
- One pair size 19 (15mm) needles, *or size to obtain gauge*
- One size P/Q (15mm) crochet hook
- Contrasting scrap yarn
- Locking stitch markers

GAUGE

8 sts and 11 rows to 4"/10cm over chart, after blocking, using size 19 (15mm) needles. *TAKE TIME TO CHECK GAUGE.*

NOTES

1) Stitch pattern is based on #70 Right Rhombus (see page 103).

2) Locking stitch markers in rows 2 and 20 are left until finishing, when 2 hand-sewn tucks are worked to maintain pattern across grafted rows.

3) Rhombus pattern can be worked from written instructions or chart, working all Dimensional Tucks using the standard ON WS method.

COWL

Using the provisional cast-on (see page 180), cast on 27 sts.

Work rows 1–14, rep rows 3–14 six times more, then work rows 15–23.

Do *not* bind off.

FINISHING

Carefully remove scrap yarn from provisional cast-on. Graft first row to last row using Kitchener Stitch (see page 180).

To maintain rhombus pat across grafted rows, work as foll:

Thread yarn needle with length of yarn approx 5"/12.5cm long. With WS facing, draw yarn through both legs of left marked st in row 20, remove marker, then draw yarn through both legs of left marked st in row 2 and remove marker. Draw yarn up tightly and tie. Rep with right marked sts in rows 20 and 2.

Weave in ends. Block to measurements. ◆

RHOMBUS PATTERN

(over 27 sts)

Row 1 (RS) Knit.

Row 2 Sl 1, k1, p1, k1, p3, k1 (pm in this st), p11, k1, p3, k1 (pm in this st), p1, k2.

Rows 3, 5, 7, 9, 11, and 13 Sl 1, k to end.

Rows 4, 6, 10, and 12 Sl 1, k1, p to last 2 sts, k2.

Row 8 Sl 1, k1, p5, RTT, p3, k1, p3, LTT, p3, k1, p5, k2.

Row 14 Sl 1, k1, p1, k1, p3, LTT, p11, k1, p3, RTT, p1, k2.

Rows 15, 17, 19, and 21 Sl 1, k to end.

Rows 16 and 18 Sl 1, k1, p to last 2 sts, k2.

Row 20 Sl 1, k1, p5, RTT, p3, k1 (pm in this st), p3, LTT, p3, k1 (pm in this st), p5, k2.

Row 22 Sl 1, k1, p to last 2 sts, k2.

Row 23 Sl 1, k to end.

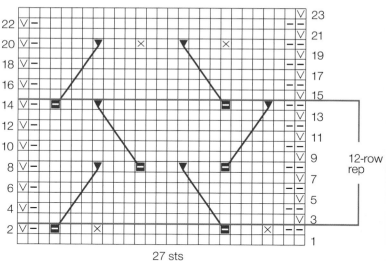

27 sts

12-row rep

Stitch Key

☐ k on RS, p on WS

⊟ k on WS

▽ sl 1

⊠ k1 and pm in st

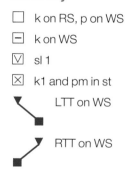

LTT on WS

RTT on WS

LUXURY FINGERLESS MITTS

Cashmere yarn brings added luxury to stylish, textured, fingerless mitts—the perfect accessory for a night out.

SKILL LEVEL
■■■□

KNITTED MEASUREMENTS

Hand circumference 7"/18cm

Length 9¼"/23.5cm

MATERIALS

- 1 1¾oz/50g ball (approx 258yd/236m) of Jade Sapphire Exotic Fibres *Aaah* (cashmere) in #04 Apparition
- **One set (4) size 5 (3.75mm) double-pointed needles (dpn),** *or size to obtain gauges*
- **Stitch markers and stitch holder**

GAUGES

- 21 sts and 36 rnds to 4"/10cm over garter st using size 5 (3.75mm) needles.
- 13 sts to 1¾"/4.5cm over either chart using size 5 (3.75mm) needles.

TAKE TIME TO CHECK GAUGES.

NOTES

1) Stitch pattern is based on #48 Wavy Braid (see page 77).

2) Work all Dimensional Tucks using the alternative FROM WS method.

LEFT MITT

Using the long-tail cast-on (see page 180), cast on 36 sts and divide evenly over 3 dpn. Join, taking care to not twist sts, and pm for beg of rnd.

Cuff

Inc rnd 1 K2, kfb, *k5, kfb; rep from * to last 3 sts, k3—42 sts.

Rnds 2–10 Knit.

Rnd 11 K3, [*drop next st off needle and allow it to run down to cast-on edge, bring RH needle down under cast-on edge to WS of work, yo, bring loop back to RS under cast-on edge and place on LH needle, knit loop, pulling tight to gather fabric*, k6] 5 times, rep between *s once more, k3.

Dec rnd 12 K3, *k2tog, k5; rep from * to last 4 sts, k2tog, k2—36 sts.

Rearrange sts so that DPN #1 and #3 have 13 sts each and DPN #2 has 10 sts.

Inc rnd 13 *DPN #1* P13; *DPN #2* K3, [M1, k2] 3 times, k1; *DPN #3* P13—39 sts (13 sts on each dpn).

Rnd 14 Knit.

Begin Chart

Note Left mitt chart is worked over DPN #2 (written chart instructions appear within parentheses).

Rnds 1, 3, 5, and 7 P13; (k6, p1, k6); p13.

Rnd 2 K13; (k6, p1, k4, p1, k1); k13.

Rnds 4 and 6 K13; (k6, p1, k6); k13.

Rnd 8 K13; (k1, p1, k4, p1, LTT, k5); k13.

Rnds 9, 11, 13, 15, and 17 P13; (k6, p1, k6); p13.

Rnds 10 and 12 K13; (k6, p1, k6); k13.

Rnd 14 K13; (k5, RTT, p1, k4, p1, k1); k13.

Rnds 16 and 18 K13; (k6, p1, k6); k13.

Rnd 19 P13; (k6, p1, k6); p13.

Rnds 20–38 Rep rnds 8–19 once more, then rep rnds 8–14 once more.

Thumb Gusset

Note Cont left mitt chart on DPN #2, beg with rnd 15 (written chart instructions appear within parentheses).

Inc rnd 39 P6, pfb, kfb, p5; (k6, p1, k6); p13—41 sts.

Rnd 40 K15; (k6, p1, k6); k13.

Inc rnd 41 P7, M1, k2, M1, p6; (k6, p1, k6); p13—43 sts.

Rnd 42 K17; (k6, p1, k6); k13.

Inc rnd 43 P7, M1, k4, M1, p6; (k6, p1, k6); p13—45 sts.

Cont to work thumb gusset over DPN #1 and rows 8–19 of left mitt chart over DPN #2 (written chart instructions appear within parentheses).

Rnd 44 K19; (k1, p1, k4, p1, LTT, k5); k13.

Inc rnd 45 P7, M1, k6, M1, p6; (k6, p1, k6); p13—47 sts.

Rnd 46 K21; (k6, p1, k6); k13.

Inc rnd 47 P7, M1, k8, M1, p6; (k6, p1, k6); p13—49 sts.

Rnd 48 K23; (k6, p1, k6); k13.

Inc rnd 49 P7, M1, k10, M1, p6; (k6, p1, k6); p13—51 sts.

Rnd 50 K25; (k5, RTT, p1, k4, p1, k1); k13.

Inc rnd 51 P7, M1, k12, M1, p6; (k6, p1, k6); p13—53 sts.

Rnd 52 K27; (k6, p1, k6); k13.

Inc rnd 53 P7, M1, k14, M1, p6; (k6, p1, k6); p13—55 sts.

Dec rnd 54 K7, place next 16 sts on st holder for thumb, cast on 2 sts, k6; (k6, p1, k6); k13—41 sts.

Dec rnd 55 P6, [p2tog] twice, p5; (k6, p1, k6); p13—39 sts.

Cont in pat, rep rnds 8–19 twice more, omitting purl Tuck Stitch in chart on rnd 14 of final rep.

Bind off rnd *DPN #1* Bind off all sts purlwise; *DPN #2* Bind off 5 sts knitwise, k2tog, then bind off that st and all rem sts knitwise; *DPN #3* Bind off all sts purlwise.

Thumb

Place 16 sts for thumb on dpn as foll: 4 sts on DPN #1, 6 sts on DPN #2, 6 sts on DPN #3. Pick up and k 4 sts along inner edge of thumb, sl to DPN #1—20 sts.

Rnd 1 Knit.

Rnds 2 and 3 [K2tog] twice, k to end.

Rnds 4 and 5 Knit.

Bind off.

RIGHT MITT

Cuff

Cast on and work rnds 1–14 of cuff as for left mitt.

Begin Chart

Note Right mitt chart is worked over DPN #2 (written chart instructions appear within parentheses).

Rnds 1, 3, 5, and 7 P13; (k6, p1, k6); p13.

Rnd 2 K13; (k1, p1, k4, p1, k6); k13.

Rnds 4 and 6 K13; (k6, p1, k6); k13.

Rnd 8 K13; (k5, RTT, p1, k4, p1, k1); k13.

Rnds 9, 11, 13, 15, and 17 P13; (k6, p1, k6); p13.

Rnds 10 and 12 K13; (k6, p1, k3); k13.

Rnd 14 K13; (k1, p1, k4, p1, LTT, k5); k13.

Rnds 16 and 18 K13; (k6, p1, k6); k13.

Rnd 19 P13; (k6, p1, k6); p13.

Rnds 20–38 Rep rnds 8–19 once more, then rep rnds 8–14 once more.

Thumb Gusset

Note Cont right mitt chart on DPN #2, beg with rnd 15 (written chart instructions appear within parentheses).

Inc rnd 39 P13; (k6, p1, k6); p5, pfb, kfb, p6—41 sts.

Rnd 40 K13; (k6, p1, k6); k13.

Inc rnd 41 P13; (k6, p1, k6); p6, M1, k2, M1, p7—43 sts.

Rnd 42 K13; (k6, p1, k6); k17.

Inc rnd 43 P13; (k6, p1, k6); p6, M1, k4, M1, p7—45 sts.

Cont to work rnds 8–19 of right mitt chart over DPN #2 (written chart instructions appear within parentheses) and thumb gusset over DPN #3.

Rnd 44 K13; (k5, RTT, p1, k4, p1, k1); k19.

Inc rnd 45 P13; (k6, p1, k6); p6, M1, k6, M1, p7—47 sts.

Rnd 46 K13; (k6, p1, k6); k21.

Inc rnd 47 P13; (k6, p1, k6); p6, M1, k8, M1, p7—49 sts.

Rnd 48 K13; (k6, p1, k6); k23.

Inc rnd 49 P13; (k6, p1, k6); p6, M1, k10, M1, p7—51 sts.

Rnd 50 K13; (k1, p1, k4, p1, LTT, k5); k25.

Inc rnd 51 P13; (k6, p1, k6); p6, M1, k12, M1, p7—53 sts.

Rnd 52 K13; (k6, p1, k6); k27.

Inc rnd 53 P13; (k6, p1, k6); p6, M1, k14, M1, p7—55 sts.

Dec rnd 54 K13; (k6, p1, k6); k6, place next 16 sts on st holder for thumb, cast on 2 sts, k7—41 sts.

Dec rnd 55 P13; (k6, p1, k6); p5, [p2tog] twice, p6—39 sts.

Complete as for left mitt.

FINISHING

Weave in ends. Block to measurements. ◆

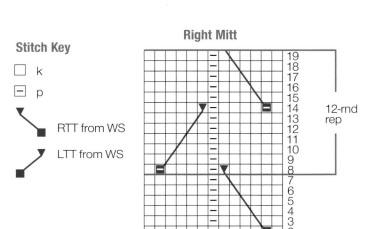

Left Mitt

19 18 17 16 15 14 13 12 11 10 9 8 7 6 5 4 3 2 1

12-rnd rep

13 sts

Stitch Key

☐ k

⊟ p

RTT from WS

LTT from WS

Right Mitt

19 18 17 16 15 14 13 12 11 10 9 8 7 6 5 4 3 2 1

12-rnd rep

13 sts

DREAMWEAVER COWL

A continuous field of weave-inspired Dimensional Tucks creates a dream of incredible softness and lightness in baby alpaca.

SKILL LEVEL
■■■□

KNITTED MEASUREMENTS

Circumference approx 21"/53.5cm

Height 7"/18cm

MATERIALS

• 2 1¾oz/50g hanks (each approx 110yd/100m) of Blue Sky Fibers *Baby Alpaca* (baby alpaca) in #808 Avocado

• One size 5 (3.75mm) circular needle, 16"/40cm long,

or size to obtain gauge

• Stitch marker

GAUGE

20 sts and 28 rnds to 4"/10cm over dreamweaver pat, after blocking, using size 5 (3.75mm) needle.

TAKE TIME TO CHECK GAUGE.

NOTES

1) Stitch pattern is based on #81 Tight Weave (see page 119).

2) Dreamweaver pattern can be worked from written instructions or chart, working all Dimensional Tucks using the alternative FROM WS method.

DREAMWEAVER PATTERN

(multiple of 8 sts plus 8 sts)

Rnd 1 K6, *p1, k7; rep from * to last 2 sts, p1, k1.

Rnds 2–6 Knit.

Rnd 7 K2, LTT, k3, *p1, k3, LTT, k3; rep from * to last 2 sts, p1, k1.

Rnds 8–12 Knit.

Note Tuck Stitch for first RTT of rnd 13 is on other side of beg of rnd marker.

Rnd 13 K2, RTT, k3, *p1, k3, RTT, k3; rep from * to last 2 sts, p1, k1.

Rnds 14–18 Knit.

Rep rnds 7–18 for dreamweaver pat.

COWL

Using the I-cord cast-on, cast on until 140 sts. Bind off 4 sts, leaving a tail long enough to later seam tog the ends of the cast-on I-cord—136 sts.

Join, taking care to not twist sts, and pm for beg of rnd.

Begin Pattern

Work rnds 1–18 of pat once, rnds 7–18 five times more, then rnd 7 once more, omitting purl Tuck Stitches on final rnd 7.

FINISHING

Bind off using I-cord bind-off. Sew edges of I-cord bind-off tog. Sew edges of I-cord cast-on tog. Weave in ends. Block to measurements. ◆

I-CORD CAST-ON

1) Cast on 4 sts using the long-tail cast-on (see page 180). Slip 4 sts on RH needle to LH needle so first cast-on st is at tip of LH needle.

2) Pull yarn snugly across back of work, kfb, k3.

3) Slip 4 sts to LH needle.

Rep steps 2 and 3 until desired number of sts are cast on.

I-CORD BIND-OFF

1) Cast on 4 sts using the knitted cast-on.

2) K3, k2tog tbl (last cast-on st and next st on needle).

3) Slip sts from RH needle to LH needle.

4) Pull yarn snugly across back of work, k3, k2tog tbl.

Rep steps 3 and 4 to last 4 sts. Bind off rem sts using the basic knitted bind-off.

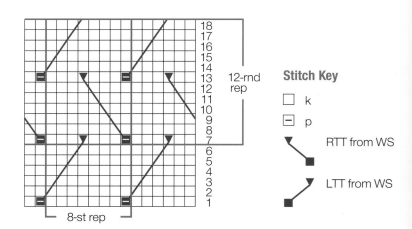

STACKED FLAMES
SCARF

This scarf staggers a unique Dimensional Tuck for an extra-wide scarf that offers extra warmth and extra style.

SKILL LEVEL

■■■□

KNITTED MEASUREMENTS

6½ x 72"/16.5 x 183cm

MATERIALS

• 4 1¾oz/50g skeins (each approx 110yd/100m) of Noro

Silk Garden (silk/mohair/lambswool) in #269 White/Natural

• **One pair size 9 (5.5mm) needles, *or size to obtain gauge***

GAUGE

19 sts and 23 rows to 4"/10cm over chart, after blocking, using size 9 (5.5mm) needles.

TAKE TIME TO CHECK GAUGE.

NOTES

1) Stitch pattern is based on #22 Flame (see page 53).

2) Flame pattern can be worked from written instructions or chart, working all Dimensional Tucks using the alternative ON RS method.

SCARF

Cast on 31 sts.

Work rows 1–20, work rows 9–20 thirty-two times more, then work

rows 21–27.

Bind off.

FINISHING

Weave in ends. Block to measurements. ◆

FLAME PATTERN

(over 31 sts)

Row 1 (RS) P3, k11, p3, k11, p3.

Row 2 and all WS rows K1, sl 1 wyif, k1, p11, k1, sl 1 wyif, k1,

p11, k1, sl 1 wyif, k1.

Row 3 P3, k11, p3, k1, p1, k7, p1, k1, p3.

Rows 5 and 7 P3, k11, p3, k11, p3.

Row 9 P3, k1, p1, k7, p1, k1, p3, k5, LRTT, k5, p3.

Rows 11 and 13 P3, k11, p3, k11, p3.

Row 15 P3, k5, LRTT, k5, p3, k1, p1, k7, p1, k1, p3.

Rows 17 and 19 P3, k11, p3, k11, p3.

Row 21 P3, k1, p1, k7, p1, k1, p3, k5, LRTT, k5, p3.

Rows 23 and 25 P3, k11, p3, k11, p3.

Row 27 P3, k5, LRTT, k5, p3, k11, p3.

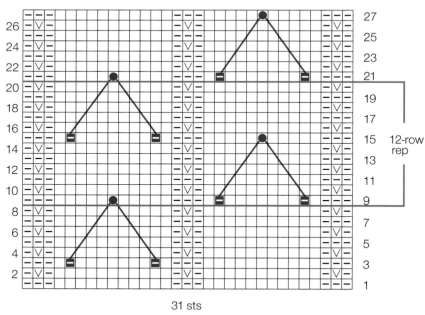

31 sts

12-row rep

Stitch Key

☐ k on RS, p on WS

⊟ p on RS, k on WS

⊻ sl 1 wyif

● LRTT on RS

LUCKY HAT

Forget the cable needle and whip up these faux horseshoe cables in a jiffy for extra-squishy texture.

SKILL LEVEL
■ ■ ■ □

KNITTED MEASUREMENTS

Brim circumference (slightly stretched) 17"/43cm

Length 11½"/29cm

MATERIALS

• 2 1¾oz/50g balls (each approx 110yd/100m) of Debbie Bliss *Rialto DK* (extra fine merino) each in #04 Grey (A) and #57 Banana (B)

• One each sizes 6 and 9 (4 and 5.5mm) circular needles, 16"/40cm long, *or size to obtain gauge*

• One set (5) size 6 (4mm) double-pointed needles (dpn)

• Stitch markers

GAUGE

26 sts and 32 rnds to 4"/10cm over chart, after blocking, using size 6 (4mm) needle.

TAKE TIME TO CHECK GAUGE.

NOTES

1) Stitch pattern is based on #34 Upward Horseshoe (see page 64).

2) Hat is worked in the round, working all Dimensional Tucks using the alternative FROM WS method.

Rnds 10 and 12 Knit.

Rnd 13 *K14, p4; rep from * around.

Rep rnds 2–13 five times more.

Crown Shaping

Rnd 1 *K14, p4; rep from * around.

Rnd 2 Knit.

Dec rnd 3 *K14, [p2tog] twice; rep from * around—128 sts.

Rnd 4 Knit.

Rnd 5 *K14, p2; rep from * around.

Dec rnd 6 *Ssk, k10, k2tog, k2; rep from * around—112 sts.

Rnd 7 *K12, p2; rep from * around.

Dec rnd 8 *Ssk, k8, k2tog, k2; rep from * around—96 sts.

Dec rnd 9 *K3, ssk, k2tog, k3, p2; rep from * around—80 sts.

Dec rnd 10 *[Ssk, k1] twice, k2tog, k2; rep from * around—56 sts.

Dec rnd 11 *Ssk, k1, k2tog, p2; rep from * around—40 sts.

Dec rnd 12 *K3tog, k2; rep from * around—24 sts.

Dec rnd 13 *K2tog; rep from * around—12 sts.

Cut yarn, leaving a 6"/15.5cm tail. Draw tail through rem sts and secure.

FINISHING

Weave in ends. Block to measurements.

With B, make large pompom and secure to top of crown. ◆

HAT

With larger needle and 2 strands of B held tog, cast on 72 sts. Join, taking care to not twist sts, and pm for beg of rnd.

Rnds 1–8 *K2, p2; rep from * around.

Cut B and join a single strand of A. Change to smaller needle.

Set-up rnd *Knit into each individual strand of next st; rep from * around—144 sts.

Begin Chart

Rnd 1 *K14, p4; rep from * around.

Rnd 2 *K1, p1, k10, p1, k5; rep from * around.

Rnds 3, 5, and 7 *K14, p4; rep from * around.

Rnds 4 and 6 Knit.

Rnd 8 *K5, RTT, k2, LTT, k9; rep from * around.

Rnds 9 and 11 *K14, p4; rep from * around.

Stitch Key

☐ k

⊟ p

RTT from WS

LTT from WS

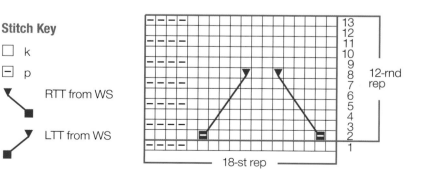

18-st rep

12-rnd rep

FRONT & CENTER SWEATER

Combining easy style with a bold front panel, this project uses engaging construction techniques for a sweater that is as fun to wear as it is to knit.

SKILL LEVEL
■ ■ ■ ■

SIZES

For women's sizes Small (Medium, Large, and X-Large). Shown in size Small.

KNITTED MEASUREMENTS

Bust 41½ (46½, 49½, 54½)"/105.5 (118, 125.5, 138.5)cm

Length 22¼ (22¾, 23¾, 24½)"/56.5 (58, 60.5, 62)cm

Upper arm 14½ (15¼, 16¼, 17)"/37 (38.5, 41, 43)cm

MATERIALS

• 6 (6, 7, 7) 1¾oz/50g skeins (each approx 160yd/146m) of HiKoo/Skacel Collection *Kenzie* (New Zealand merino/nylon/angora/alpaca/silk noils) in #1002 Grey Salt (A) 〔4〕

• 2 (2, 3, 3) skeins in #1018 Grey Seal (B)

• 1 3½oz/100g hank (approx 208yd/187m) of HiKoo/Skacel Collection *Kenzington* (New Zealand merino/nylon/alpaca/silk noils) in #1015 Boysenberry (C) 〔5〕

• One size 6 (4mm) circular needle, 40"/100cm long, *or size to obtain gauges*

• One pair each sizes 10 and 10½ (6 and 6.5mm) needles

• One size 10½ (6.5mm) circular needle, 16"/40cm long

• One size G/6 (4mm) crochet hook and contrasting scrap yarn

• Stitch markers and stitch holders

GAUGES

• 17 sts and 26 rows to 4"/10cm over St st and *Kenzie*, after blocking, using size 6 (4mm) needle.

• Approx 23½ sts and 24 rows to 4"/10cm over center panel and *Kenzington*, after blocking, using size 10½ (6.5mm) needles.

TAKE TIME TO CHECK GAUGES.

NOTES FOR CENTER PANEL

1) Center panel can be worked from written instructions or chart. Set-up rows are not shown on chart.

2) Slip first 2 and last 2 sts with yarn in front on every WS row for selvage sts.

3) For center panel, LRTT is worked using two methods: LRTT on WS (blue symbols on chart) and LRTT from RS (red symbols on chart).

4) Stitch pattern is based on #24 Lyre Panel (see page 57).

CENTER PANEL

Using size 10½ (6.5mm) needles and C, cast on 41 sts.

Set-up row 1 (WS) P2, k1, p35, k1, p2.

Set-up row 2 K2, p1, k35, p1, k2.

Set-up row 3 Sl 2 wyif, k1, p35, k1, sl 2 wyif.

For Sizes LARGE AND X-LARGE Only

Rep set-up rows 2 and 3 once more.

Begin Pattern

Row 1 and all RS rows K2, p1, k35, p1, k2.

Row 2 Sl 2 wyif, k1, p1, [k1, p7, k1, p3] twice, k1, p7, k1, p1, k1, sl 2 wyif.

Rows 4 and 6 Sl 2 wyif, k1, p35, k1, sl 2 wyif.

Row 8 Sl 2 wyif, k1, p5, LRTT on WS, p11, LRTT from RS, p11, LRTT on WS, p5, k1, sl 2 wyif.

Rows 10 and 12 Sl 2 wyif, k1, p35, k1, sl 2 wyif.

Row 14 Rep row 2.

Rows 16 and 18 Sl 2 wyif, k1, p35, k1, sl 2 wyif.

Row 20 Sl 2 wyif, k1, p5, LRTT from RS, p11, LRTT on WS, p11, LRTT from RS, p5, k1, sl 2 wyif.

Rows 22 and 24 Sl 2 wyif, k1, p35, k1, sl 2 wyif.

Rep rows 1–24 three times more, then rep rows 1–12 once more. Bind off.

BODY

Note Circular needle is used to accommodate large number of sts. Do *not* join.

With A, size 6 (4mm) needle, and using the provisional cast-on (see page 180), cast on 159 (179, 195, 215) sts.

Work in St st (k on RS, p on WS) for 13 (13½, 14, 14½)"/33 (34.5, 35.5, 37)cm, end with a RS row.

Armhole Shaping

Next row (WS) P28 (32, 36, 40) for left front, bind off 10 (12, 12, 14) sts, p until there are 83 (91, 99, 107) sts after bind-off for back, bind off 10 (12, 12, 14) sts, p28 (32, 36, 40) for right front.

Cut yarn. Place each group of sts on a separate st holder.

SLEEVES

Note Cuff is worked with 2 strands of yarn held tog. When cuff is complete, remainder of sleeve is worked with a single strand.

With size 10 (6mm) needles and 2 strands of A held tog, cast on 37 (41, 45, 49) sts.

Row 1 K1, *p2, k2; rep from * to end.

Row 2 *P2, k2; rep from * to last st, p1.

Rep rows 1 and 2 for k2, p2 ribbing for 2"/5cm. Cut one strand of yarn.

Change to size 6 (4mm) needle.

Work 10 rows in St st.

Inc row (RS) K1, M1, k to last st, M1, k1—2 sts inc'd.

Rep inc row every 4th row 5 times, then every 6th row 8 times—65 (69, 73, 77) sts.

Cont in St st until piece measures approx 19"/48cm from beg, end with WS row.

Next row (RS) Bind off 5 (6, 6, 7) sts, work to last 5 (6, 6, 7) sts, bind off rem sts.

Cut yarn. Place rem 55 (57, 61, 63) sts on st holder. Rep for 2nd sleeve.

YOKE

Next row (RS) With size 6 (4mm) circular needle and B, k28 (32, 36, 40) for right front, pm, k55 (57, 61, 63) sleeve sts, pm, k83 (91, 99, 107) for back, pm, k55 (57, 61, 63) sleeve sts, pm, k28 (32, 36, 40) for left front—249 (269, 293, 313) sts.

Next row Purl, slipping markers.

Dec row 1 (RS) [K to 3 sts before marker, k2tog, p1, sm, ssk, k to 2 sts before marker, k2tog, sm, p1, ssk] twice, k to end—8 sts dec'd.

Next row [P to 1 st before marker, k1, sm, p to next marker, sm, k1] twice, p to end.

Rep last 2 rows 7 (9, 14, 15) times more—185 (189, 173, 185) sts.

For Size MEDIUM Only

Dec row 2 (RS) K to 1 st before marker, p1, sm, ssk, k to 2 sts before marker, k2tog, sm, p1, ssk, k to 3 sts before marker, k2tog, p1, sm, ssk, k to 2 sts before marker, k2tog, sm, p1, k to end—6 sts dec'd.

Next row [P to 1 st before marker, k1, sm, p to next marker, sm, k1] twice, p to end.

Rep last 2 rows once more—177 sts.

For All Sizes

Dec row 3 (RS) [K to 1 st before marker, p1, sm, ssk, k to 2 sts before marker, k2tog, sm, p1] twice, k to end—4 sts dec'd.

Next row [P to 1 st before marker, k1, sm, p to next marker, sm, k1] twice, p to end.

Rep last 2 rows 7 (3, 2, 2) times more, then rep dec row 3 once more—149 (157, 157, 169) sts.

Add Center Panel and Begin Saddle Shaping

With RS facing, pick up sts across top of center panel below bind-off as foll: pick up and k 1 st in each knit st of center panel, skipping the two purl sts—39 sts.

Turn. Center panel and yoke sts are now all on size 6 (4mm) needle.

Next row (WS) P1, p2tog, [p2tog, p1] 10 times, [p2tog] 3 times—there are 25 sts over center panel, pm, p to 2 sts before marker, p3tog (removing marker), p19 (21, 21, 21), p3tog (removing marker). Turn.

Short-Row Left Saddle-Shoulder Shaping

Short row 1 (RS) Sl 1 wyib, k19 (21, 21, 21), sssk. Turn.

Short row 2 (WS) Sl 1 wyif, p19 (21, 21, 21), p3tog. Turn.

Rep short rows 1 and 2 ten times more, do *not* turn on final short row 2. Purl across back sts to 2 sts before next sleeve marker, p3tog (removing marker), p19 (21, 21, 21), p3tog (removing marker). Turn.

Short-Row Right Saddle-Shoulder Shaping

Short row 1 (RS) Sl 1 wyib, k19 (21, 21, 21), SK2P. Turn.

Short row 2 (WS) Sl 1 wyif, p19 (21, 21, 21), p3tog. Turn.

Rep short rows 1 and 2 ten times more—78 (86, 86, 98) sts.

COLLAR

Change to size 10½ (6.5mm) needle, join 2nd strand of B, and pm for beg of rnd. Dec 0 (2, 2, 2) sts on first rnd, work in k3, p3 rib until collar measures 4"/10cm—78 (84, 86, 96) sts. Bind off in pat.

FINISHING

Sew sides of center panel to front edges of body, sewing approx 2 body rows to every panel row and easing to fit, if necessary.

Sew sleeve and underarm seams.

Hem

Carefully remove scrap yarn from provisional cast-on, placing released sts on size 6 (4mm) needle—159 (179, 195, 215) sts. With RS facing and A, pick up and k 39 sts evenly along lower edge of center panel—198 (218, 234, 254). Knit around to sts along lower edge of center panel, pm to mark beg of rnd.

Next rnd Dec along center panel as foll: k1, k2tog, [k2tog, k1] 10 times, [k2tog] 3 times; k to end of rnd—184 (204, 220, 240) sts.

Work in St st (k every rnd) until hem measures 1½"/4cm from lower edge of center panel. Purl 1 rnd. Cont in St st until hem measures 1½"/4cm from purl rnd. Bind off. Fold hem at purl rnd and sew in place.

Weave in ends. Block to measurements. ◆

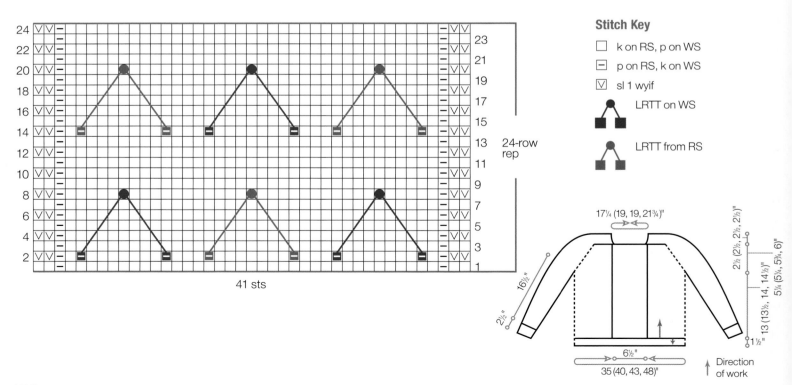

Stitch Key

☐ k on RS, p on WS

⊟ p on RS, k on WS

☑ sl 1 wyif

LRTT on WS

LRTT from RS

24-row rep

41 sts

17¼ (19, 19, 21¾)"

2½ (2½, 2½, 2½)"

13 (13½, 14, 14½)"

5¼ (5¼, 5¾, 6)"

16½"

2½"

1½"

6½"

35 (40, 43, 48)"

Direction of work

TUCKS GALORE BLANKET

Cuddle up with the ultimate sampler of more than 20 different Dimensional Tuck stitch patterns.

Knit each square separately, sew them together, then pick up stitches along the edge for a border worked in the round.

SKILL LEVEL
■■■□

KNITTED MEASUREMENTS

36 x 45" (91.5 x 114.5cm)

MATERIALS

• 24 1¾oz/50g balls (each approx 65yd/60m) of Debbie Bliss *Rialto Chunky* (extra fine merino) in #43010 Duck Egg ⑤

• One pair size 10½ (6.5mm) needles, *or size to obtain gauge*

• Two size 10½ (6.5mm) circular needles, each 40"/100cm long

• Stitch markers

GAUGE

15 sts and 28 rows to 4"/10cm over garter st, after blocking, using size 10½ (6.5mm) needles.

TAKE TIME TO CHECK GAUGE.

NOTES

1) Circular needles are used for border only.

2) Work each individual square, sew all squares together, then work border as instructed.

CHART A

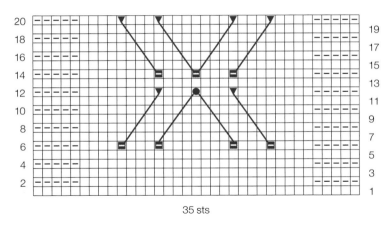

35 sts

SQUARE A

Note Pattern is based on #86 Center Diamond with Outward Arrows (see page 125).

Cast on 35 sts.

Beg with a RS row, knit 16 rows.

Work chart A as foll: work rows 1–20, then work rows 1–5 once more.

Beg with a WS row, knit 15 rows.

Bind off.

CHART B

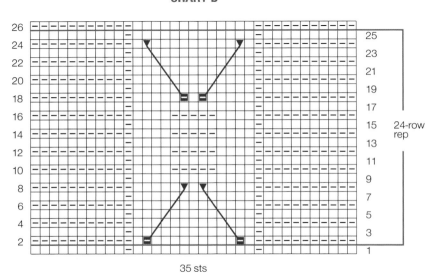

35 sts

SQUARE B

Note Pattern is based on #13 Long Chain with Center Garter (see page 41).

Cast on 35 sts.

Beg with a WS row, knit 3 rows.

Work chart B as foll: work row 1, work rows 2–25 twice, then work row 26.

Beg with a RS row, knit 3 rows.

Bind off.

CHART C

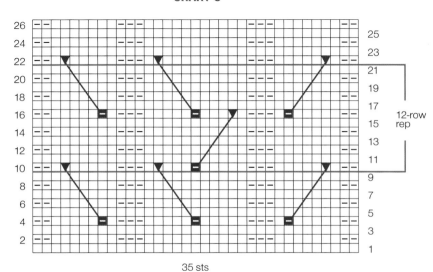

35 sts

SQUARE C

Note Pattern is based on #49 Basic Upward Braid (see page 79), #45 Simple Left Twist (see page 75), and #46 Simple Right Twist (see page 75).

Cast on 35 sts.

Beg with a WS row, knit 3 rows.

Work chart C as foll: work rows 1–9, work rows 10–21 three times, then work rows 22–26.

Beg with a RS row, knit 3 rows.

Bind off.

SQUARE D

Note Pattern is based on #9 Chain Link (see page 37).

Cast on 35 sts.

Beg with a WS row, knit 3 rows.

Work chart D as foll: work rows 1–4, work rows 5–24 twice, then work rows 25–30.

Beg with a RS row, knit 3 rows.

Bind off.

SQUARE E

Note Pattern is based on #67 Bowties and Tietacks (see page 99).

Cast on 35 sts.

Beg with a WS row, knit 3 rows.

Work chart E as foll: work row 1, work rows 2–20 twice, then work rows 22–30.

Beg with a RS row, knit 3 rows.

Bind off.

SQUARE F

Note Pattern is based on #22 Flame (see page 53), working all Dimensional Tucks using the alternative ON RS method.

Cast on 35 sts.

Beg with a WS row, knit 3 rows.

Work chart F as foll: work rows 1–4, then work rows 5–16 four times.

Beg with a RS row, knit 3 rows.

Bind off.

Stitch Key

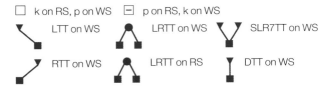

☐ k on RS, p on WS   ⊟ p on RS, k on WS

LTT on WS   LRTT on WS   SLR7TT on WS

RTT on WS   LRTT on RS   DTT on WS

CHART D

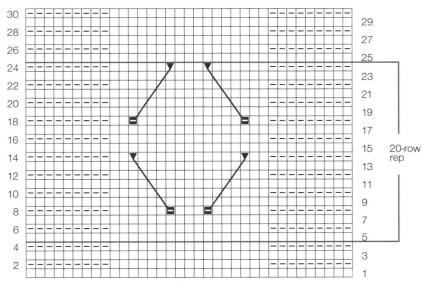

35 sts

CHART E

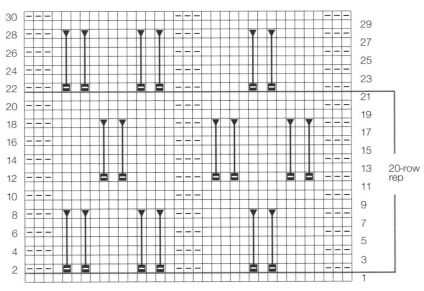

35 sts

CHART F

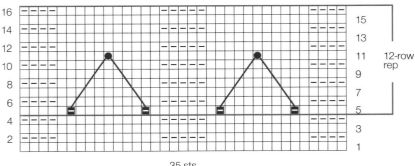

35 sts

CHART G

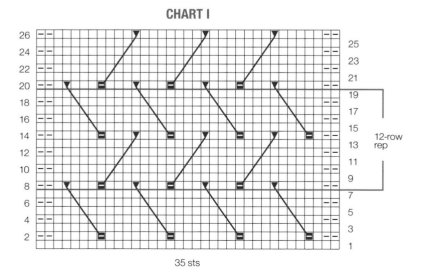

35 sts

12-row rep

SQUARE G

Note Pattern is based on #36 Upward Shells with Twists (page 65).

Cast on 35 sts.

Beg with a WS row, knit 3 rows.

Work chart G as foll: work rows 1–7, work rows 8–19 three times, then work rows 20–26.

Beg with a RS row, knit 3 rows.

Bind off.

CHART H

35 sts

24-row rep

SQUARE H

Note Pattern is based on #59 Simple Right Twist with Alternating Stitches (see page 89).

Cast on 35 sts.

Beg with a WS row, knit 3 rows.

Work chart H as foll: work rows 1 and 2, then work rows 3–26 twice.

Beg with a RS row, knit 3 rows.

Bind off.

CHART I

35 sts

12-row rep

SQUARE I

Note Pattern is based on #81 Tight Weave (see page 119).

Cast on 35 sts.

Beg with a WS row, knit 3 rows.

Work chart I as foll: work rows 1–7, work rows 8–19 three times, then work rows 20–26.

Beg with a RS row, knit 3 rows.

Bind off.

SQUARE J

Note Pattern is based on #15 Twists with Diamonds (see page 43).

Cast on 35 sts.

Beg with a WS row, knit 3 rows.

Work chart J as foll: work rows 1–32, then work rows 1–18 once more.

Beg with a RS row, knit 3 rows.

Bind off.

SQUARE K

Note Pattern is based on #47 Double S-Rope (see page 76).

Cast on 35 sts.

Beg with a WS row, knit 3 rows.

Work chart K as foll: work rows 1–20 twice, then work rows 21–30.

Beg with a RS row, knit 3 rows.

Bind off.

SQUARE L

Note Pattern is based on #23 Smoke (page 53).

Cast on 35 sts.

Beg with a WS row, knit 3 rows.

Work chart L as foll: work rows 1—10 five times.

Beg with a RS row, knit 3 rows.

Bind off.

Stitch Key

□ k on RS, p on WS   ⊟ p on RS, k on WS

LTT on WS   LRTT on WS

RTT on WS

CHART J

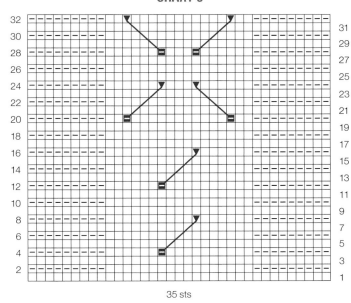

35 sts

CHART K

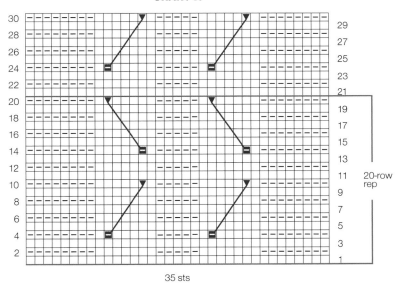

20-row rep

35 sts

CHART L

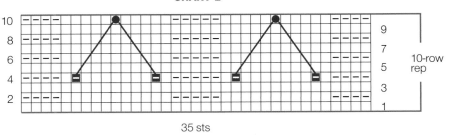

10-row rep

35 sts

CHART M

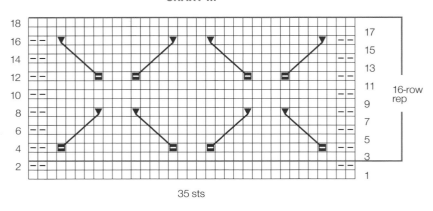

35 sts

16-row rep

SQUARE M

Note Pattern is based on #11 Chain Link Panel (see page 39).

Cast on 35 sts.

Beg with a WS row, knit 3 rows.

Work chart M as foll: work rows 1 and 2, then work rows 3–18 three times.

Beg with a RS row, knit 3 rows.

Bind off.

CHART N

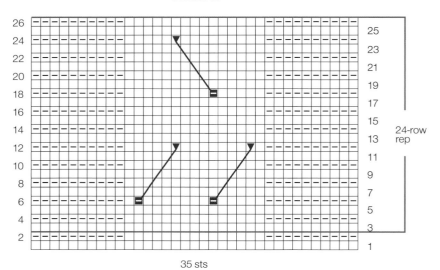

35 sts

24-row rep

SQUARE N

Note Pattern is based on #57 Plaited (see page 87).

Cast on 35 sts.

Beg with a WS row, knit 3 rows.

Work chart N as foll: work rows 1 and 2, then work rows 3–26 twice.

Beg with a RS row, knit 3 rows.

Bind off.

CHART O

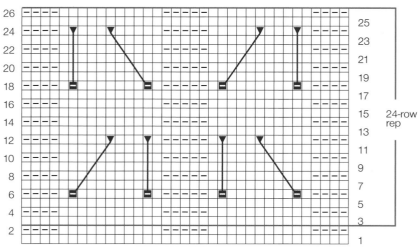

35 sts

24-row rep

SQUARE O

Note Pattern is based on #42 Alternating Check Marks (see page 71).

Cast on 35 sts.

Beg with a WS row, knit 3 rows.

Work chart O as foll: work rows 1 and 2, then work rows 3–26 twice.

Beg with a RS row, knit 3 rows.

Bind off.

SQUARE P

Note Pattern is based on #19 Gathered Ribbon (see page 49), #45 Simple Left Twist (see page 75), and #46 Simple Right Twist (see page 75).

Cast on 35 sts.

Beg with a WS row, knit 3 rows.

Work rows 1–50 of Chart P.

Beg with a RS row, knit 3 rows.

Bind off.

SQUARE Q

Note Pattern is based on #62 Upward Tweed (see page 93)

Cast on 35 sts.

Beg with a WS row, knit 3 rows.

Work chart Q as foll: work rows 1–9, work rows 10–21 twice, then work rows 22–38.

Beg with a RS row, knit 3 rows.

Bind off.

Stitch Key

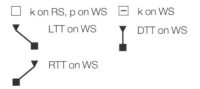

- ☐ k on RS, p on WS
- ⊟ k on WS
- LTT on WS
- DTT on WS
- RTT on WS

CHART P

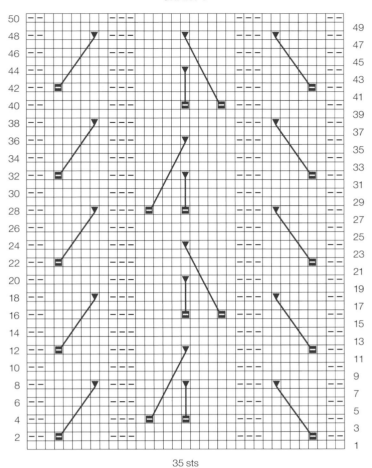

35 sts

CHART Q

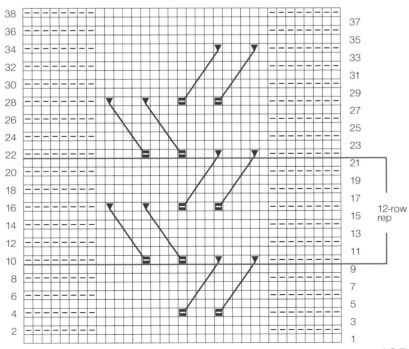

35 sts

165

CHART R

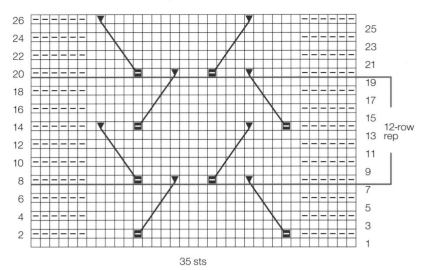

35 sts

12-row rep

CHART S

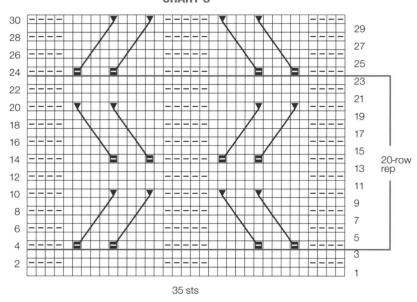

35 sts

20-row rep

CHART T

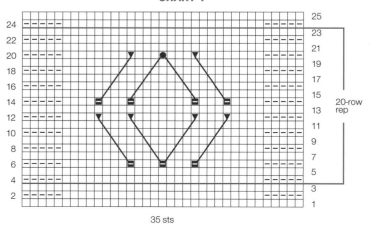

35 sts

20-row rep

SQUARE R

Note Pattern is based on #71 Left Rhombus (see page 103).

Cast on 35 sts.

Beg with a WS row, knit 3 rows.

Work chart R as foll: work rows 1–7, work rows 8–19 three times, then work rows 20–26.

Beg with a RS row, knit 3 rows.

Bind off.

SQUARE S

Note Pattern is based on #80 Interlocking Links (see page 117).

Cast on 35 sts.

Beg with a WS row, knit 3 rows.

Work chart S as foll: work rows 1–3, work rows 4–23 twice, then work rows 24–30.

Beg with a RS row, knit 3 rows.

Bind off.

SQUARE T

Note Pattern is based on #88 Ribbons and Bows (see page 129).

Cast on 35 sts.

Beg with a WS row, knit 3 rows.

Work chart T as foll: work rows 1–3, work rows 4–23 twice, then work rows 24 and 25.

Beg with a RS row, knit 3 rows.

Bind off.

Stitch Key

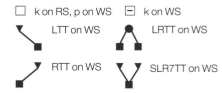

☐ k on RS, p on WS   ⊟ k on WS

▼ LTT on WS   ● LRTT on WS

RTT on WS   SLR7TT on WS

166

FINISHING

Weave in ends. Block each square to approx 8 x 8" (20.5 x 20.5cm).
Arrange squares in desired order or using assembly diagram below for
placement and sew tog.

Border

With RS facing and circular needle, beg at top left corner, *pick up
and k 2 sts in corner, pm, pick up and k 173 sts (along short side), pm,
pick up and k 2 sts in corner, pm, pick up and k 187 sts (along long
side), pm. With 2nd circular needle, rep from * once more—728 sts.
Join to work in rnds.

Rnd 1 [M1, sm, k2, sm, M1, *p1, k6; rep from * to 5 sts before
marker, p1, k4] 4 times, pm for beg of rnd.

Rnds 2–6 [Knit to marker, M1, sm, k2, sm, M1] 4 times, knit to marker.

NOTE Remove markers in next rnd except beg of rnd marker.

Rnd 7 K6, [M1, k2, M1, k10, *RTT from WS, k6; rep from * to end of
side] 4 times.

NOTE Last 6 sts are worked beyond beg of rnd marker.

Bind off as foll: K2, *sl 2 sts back to LH needle, k2tog tbl, k1; rep from
* to last 2 sts, sl last 2 sts back to LH needle, k2tog tbl and fasten off
last st. ◆

ASSEMBLY DIAGRAM

A	B	C	D	E
F	G	H	I	J
K	L	M	N	O
P	Q	R	S	T

167

TAPESTRY PONCHO

Wear a stylish tapestry of staggered patterns, knit in super baby alpaca for a soft and light fabric.

SKILL LEVEL
■■■□

KNITTED MEASUREMENTS

Width approx 32"/81cm

Length 22"/56cm

MATERIALS

• 15 .88oz/25g balls (each approx 95yd/87m) of Hikoo *SimpliCria* (super baby alpaca) in #253

• Two size 10 (6mm) circular needles, 16"/40cm and 40"/100cm long, *or size to obtain gauge*

• Stitch markers

GAUGE

19 sts and 36 rows to 4"/10cm over chart 1, after blocking, using size 10 (6mm) needle. *TAKE TIME TO CHECK GAUGE.*

NOTES

1) Stitch patterns are based on #68 Bowties and Tietacks Panel (see page 99), #80 Interlocking Links (see page 117), #38 Upward Staghorn (see page 67), and #65 Rope (see page 65).

2) Circular needle is used to accommodate large number of sts. Do *not* join, unless otherwise instructed.

3) Poncho is worked in one piece from lower front edge to shoulder, then from shoulder to lower back edge.

4) When working charts 1, 2, and 4, work 20-st rep as many times as instructed. When working chart 3, work rows 1–7 once, then rep rows 8–19 as many times as instructed, end with rows 20–28.

5) Stitch markers are placed between individual stitch patterns.

6) All Dimensional Tucks are worked using the standard ON WS method.

FRONT

With longer circular needle, cast on 166 sts.

Front Border

Row 1 (WS) Knit.

Row 2 K1, *sl 1 wyib, k1; rep from * to last st, k1.

Row 3 K1, *sl 1 wyif, k1; rep from * to last st, k1.

Rep rows 2 and 3 four times more, dec 1 st in center of last WS row—165 sts.

Begin Charts

Row 1 (RS) K1, [sl 1 wyib, k1] 3 times, k1 (8-st border), pm; work row 1 of chart 1 over 45 sts, working the first 5 sts of chart once and then the 8-st rep 5 times, pm; work row 1 of chart 2 over 16 sts, pm; work row 1 of chart 3 over

27 sts, pm; work row 1 of chart 4 over 16 sts, pm; work row 1 of chart 1 over 45 sts as before, pm; k1, [sl 1 wyib, k1] 3 times, k1 (8-st border).

Row 2 (WS) K1, [sl 1 wyif, k1] 3 times, k1, sm; work row 2 of chart 1, working 8-st rep 5 times and then rem 5 sts once, sm; work row 2 of chart 4, sm; work row 2 of chart 3, sm; work row 2 of chart 2, sm; work row 2 of chart 1 over 45 sts as before, sm; k1, [sl 1 wyif, k1] 3 times, k1.

Cont in chart pats as established, working until the 20-row reps of charts 1, 2, and 4 have been worked 7 times, then rows 1–8 once more, and for chart 3, rows 1–7 have been worked once, then the 12-row rep 11 times, then rows 20–28 once—there is a total of 148 rows above border.

NECK SHAPING

Note Discontinue center chart 3 and work these sts as described below.

Next row (RS) K1, [sl 1 wyib, k1] 3 times, k1 (8-st border), sm; work row 9 of chart 1 as established, sm; work row 9 of chart 2 as established, sm; k4, join 2nd ball of yarn and bind off center 19 sts, k to marker, sm; work row 9 of chart 4 as established, sm; work row 9 of chart 1 as established, sm; k1, [sl 1 wyib, k1] 3 times, k1 (8-st border).

Next row (WS) Work in pat to last 4 sts of right side, [p2tog] twice, pass first st over 2nd st and off needle, then work left side as foll: [p2tog] twice, pass 2nd st over first st and off needle, cont in pat to end—3 sts dec'd each side.

Next row (RS) Work in pat to last 2 sts of left side, k2tog, then work right side as foll: ssk, cont in pat to end—69 sts each side.

Work even in pat until 23 rows have been worked in the neck, or 171 rows in total above the front border.

Row 172 (WS) Work first half as foll: Work 8-st border, sm, p5, [k1, p1, k1, p5] 6 times, k1, p1, k1, p3, k2; work 2nd half as foll: K2, p3, k1, p1, k1, p5, [k1, p1, k1, p5] 6 times, sm, work 8-st border.

BACK

Note Remove all markers except first and last markers in row. All sts between border sts will now be worked in chart 1.

Next row (RS) Beg with row 13 of chart, work 69 sts of left shoulder, cast on 27 sts for back neck, then work 69 sts of right shoulder—165 sts.

Cont to work chart 1 and border sts as established until there are the same number of rows on back as on front above border, end with a WS row.

Back Border

Next row (RS) Work 8-st border, remove marker, k74, pfb, k74, remove marker, work 8-st border—166 sts.

Rep rows 2 and 3 from front border 4 times.

Knit 1 row on WS. Bind off.

NECKBAND

With RS facing and shorter circular needle, pick up and k 70 sts evenly around neck edge. Join and pm for beg of rnd.

Rnd 1 *Sl 1 wyib, k1; rep from * around.

Rnd 2 *P1, sl 1 wyib; rep from * around.

Rep rnds 1 and 2 five times more.

Bind off as foll: K2, *sl 2 sts back to LH needle, k2tog tbl, k1; rep from * around to last 2 sts, sl last 2 sts back to LH needle, k2tog tbl and fasten off last st.

FINISHING

Weave in ends. Block to measurements. ◆

CHART 2

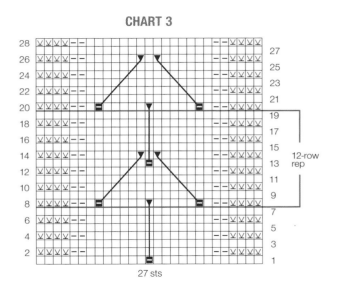

16 sts

20-row rep

CHART 3

27 sts

12-row rep

CHART 1

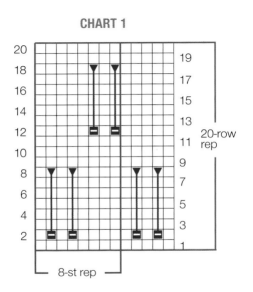

8-st rep

20-row rep

Stitch Key

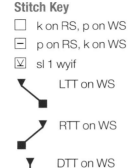

☐ k on RS, p on WS

⊟ p on RS, k on WS

☑ sl 1 wyif

▼◼ LTT on WS

◼▼ RTT on WS

▼◼ DTT on WS

CHART 4

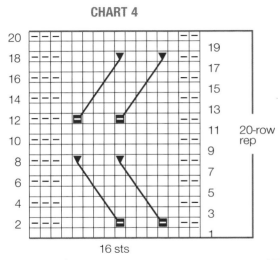

16 sts

20-row rep

RHOMBULKY
PULLOVER

This stunning pullover, worked in an exciting geometric pattern, is worked in a single piece from front to back before being seamed up each side.

SKILL LEVEL
■■■■

SIZES

For women's sizes Small/Medium (Large/X-Large). Shown in size Small/Medium.

KNITTED MEASUREMENTS

Bust 34 (45)"/86.5 (114)cm

Length 26½ (26½)"/67 (67)cm

MATERIALS

• 8 (11) 3½oz/100g skeins (each approx 126yd/115m) of Rowan *Cocoon* (merino wool/kid mohair) in #806 Frost 5

• Two size 11 (8mm) circular needles, 16"/40cm and 40"/100cm long, *or size to obtain gauge*

• Removable stitch markers

GAUGE

17 sts and 23 rows to 4"/10cm over chart using size 11 (8mm) needle.

TAKE TIME TO CHECK GAUGE.

NOTES

1) Stitch pattern is based on #72 Rhombus Panel (page 104).

2) Pullover is knit in one piece from front lower edge to shoulder to back lower edge.

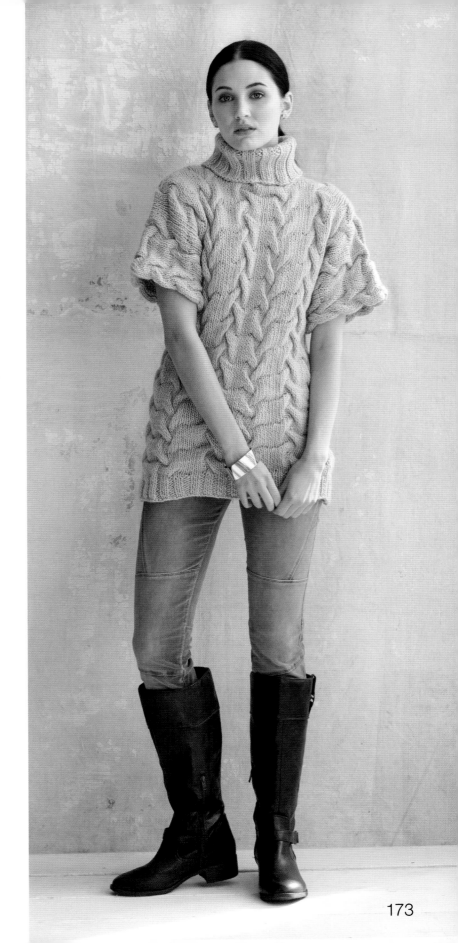

3) Schematic shows sleeve measurements before edges are folded and tacked.

4) Rhombus pattern can be worked from written instructions or chart, working all Dimensional Tucks using the standard ON WS method.

RHOMBUS PATTERN

(multiple of 24 sts plus 2 sts)

Row 1 and all RS rows Knit.

Row 2 P1, *p5, k1, p15, k1, p2; rep from * to last st, p1.

Rows 4 and 6 Purl.

Row 8 P1, *p5, k1, p3, RTT, p3, k1, p3, LTT, p6; rep from * to last st, p1.

Rows 10 and 12 Purl.

Row 14 P1, *p1, LTT, p3, k1, p11, RTT, p3, k1, p2; rep from * to last st, p1.

Rows 16 and 18 Purl.

Row 19 Knit.

Rep rows 8–19 for rhombus pat.

STITCH GLOSSARY

KSK K1, sl 1 wyib, k1.

PULLOVER

With longer circular needle, cast on 74 (98) sts.

FRONT

Row 1 P1, *k2, p2; rep from * to last st, p1.

Row 2 K1, *p2, k2; rep from * to last st, k1.

Rep rows 1 and 2 three times more for front border ribbing.

Work rows 1–19 of rhombus pat once, rep rows 8–19 five times more, then rep rows 8–18 once more.

SLEEVES

Next row (RS–pat row 19) Cast on 26 sts using the knitted cast-on, p3, k to end.

Next row (WS–pat row 8) Cast on 26 sts using the knitted cast-on, then cont in pat, working row 8 as foll: KSK, *p5, k1, p7, k1, p10*, [p5, k1, p3, RTT, p3, k1, p3, LTT, p6] 3 (4) times; rep between *s once more, KSK —126 (150) sts.

Note Single edge sts have inc'd to 3 edge sts, worked as foll: Purl 3 edge sts each side on RS rows, KSK each side on WS rows.

Beg with row 9, keeping 3 edge sts as described, cont in rhombus pat through row 19, then rep rows 8–19 twice more.

NECK SHAPING (SIZE SMALL/MEDIUM ONLY)

Note Row 8 of next pat rep omits center front Tuck Stitch.

Row 8 (WS) KSK, work 24-st rep of pat twice, p5, k1, p3, RTT, p7, LTT, p6, work 24-st rep of pat twice, KSK.

Row 9 P3, k to last 3 sts, p3.

Row 10 KSK, p to last 3 sts, KSK.

Row 11 P3, k54, join 2nd ball of yarn and bind off center 12 sts, k to last 3 sts, p3. Working both sides at once, dec 2 sts (working ssk twice) each neck edge every RS row twice, then dec 1 st each neck edge every RS row twice, ending with a pat row 19—51 sts each side.

Back Neck Joining

Row 8 (WS) Work across right shoulder sts as foll: KSK, work 24-st rep twice; using the knitted cast-on, cast on 24 sts for back neck, placing markers on the 6th and 14th cast-on sts; work across left shoulder sts as foll: work 24-st rep twice, KSK—126 sts.

Rows 9–13 Work even in pat.

Note Use marked cast-on sts as Tuck Stitches in next row.

Row 14 KSK, p1, [LTT, p3, k1, p11, RTT, p3, k1, p3] 4 times, LTT, p3, k1, p11, RTT, p3, k1, p2, KSK.

Rows 15–19 Work even in pat.

NECK SHAPING (SIZE LARGE/XLARGE ONLY)

Note Row 8 of next pat rep omits center front Tuck Stitches.

Row 8 (WS) KSK, *p5, k1, p3, RTT, p3, k1, p3, LTT, p6*; rep between *s once more, p5, k1, p3, RTT, p7, LTT, p15, RTT, p3, k1, p3, LTT, p6; rep between *s once more, p5, k1, p3, RTT, p3, k1, p3, LTT, p5, KSK.

Row 9 P3, k to last 3 sts, p3.

Row 10 KSK, p to last 3 sts, KSK.

Row 11 P3, k66, join 2nd ball of yarn, bind off center 12 sts, k to last 3 sts, p3. Working both sides at once, dec 2 sts (working ssk twice) at each neck edge every RS row twice, then dec 1 st each neck edge every RS row twice, end with a pat row 19—63 sts each side.

Back Neck Joining

Row 8 (WS) Work across right shoulder sts as foll: KSK, work 24-st rep twice, p5, k1, p3, RTT, p2; using the knitted cast-on, cast on 24 sts for back neck, placing markers on the 2nd and 18th cast-on sts; work across left shoulder sts as foll: p1, k1, p3, LTT, p6, work 24-st rep twice, KSK—150 sts.

Rows 9–13 Work even in pat.

Note Use marked cast-on sts as Tuck Stitches in next row.

Row 14 KSK, p1, [LTT, p3, k1, p11, RTT, p3, k1, p3] 5 times, LTT, p3, k1, p11, RTT, p3, k1, p1, KSK.

Rows 15–19 Work even in pat.

SLEEVES (Cont'd, Both Sizes)

Cont in rhombus pat over 126 (150) sts as before, work rows 8–19 three times.

Row 8 (WS) KSK, p9, RTT, p7, LTT, p6, work 24-st rep 3 (4) times, p9, RTT, p7, LTT, p6, KSK.

Sleeve Bind-Off

Note 3 edge sts have dec'd to 1 edge st, worked as indicated in rhombus pat and chart.

Row 9 (RS) Bind off 26 sts, k to end.

Row 10 Bind off 26 sts, p to end—74 (98) sts.

Cont in rhombus pat as for front through row 19, rep rows 8–19 six times more, then rows rep rows 8–16 once more.

Next row (RS) P3 *k2, p2; rep from * to last 3 sts, p3.

Next row K3, *p2, k2; rep from * to last 3 sts, k3.

Rep last 2 rows 3 times more for back border ribbing. Bind off in pat.

COLLAR

With RS facing and shorter circular needle, pick up and k 68 sts evenly around neck edge. Join and pm for beg of rnd.

Rnd 1 *K2, p2; rep from * around.

Rep rnd 1 until 24 rnds have been worked. Bind off in pat.

FINISHING

Sew side and underarm seams using mattress st, taking care to align pat. Fold 3 edge sts to WS of sleeves and tack in place to create scalloped edge. Weave in ends. Block to measurements. ◆

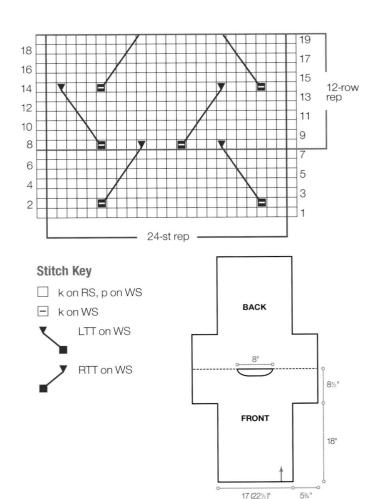

Stitch Key

☐ k on RS, p on WS

⊟ k on WS

◥ LTT on WS

◥ RTT on WS

WHISPER SHAWL

You'll love wrapping yourself in this luxurious mohair shawl, worked by first knitting a center panel, then picking up and knitting each wing separately.

SKILL LEVEL
■■■□

KNITTED MEASUREMENTS

Width (upper edge) 46"/117cm

Length (center back) 21"/53.5cm

MATERIALS

• **10 .88oz/25g balls (each approx 230yd/210m) of Rowan *Kidsilk Haze (mohair/silk) in* #600 Dewberry**

• **One pair size 10½ (6.5mm) needles, *or size to obtain gauge***

• **Stitch marker**

GAUGE

16 sts and 20 rows to 4"/10cm over chart, after blocking, using size 10½ (6.5mm) needles and 2 strands of yarn held tog.

TAKE TIME TO CHECK GAUGE.

NOTES

1) Stitch pattern is based on #49 Basic Upward Braid (page 79).

2) Shawl is worked with two strands of yarn held together throughout.

3) Begin shawl at back neck, increasing to lower back edge. Fronts are worked from stitches picked up along side edges of back piece.

4) All Dimensional Tucks are worked using the standard ON WS method.

Row 6 K3, p15, k3, p2, k7, p2, k3, p15, k3.

Row 8 K3, p15, k3, p3, k7, p3, k3, p15, k3.

Row 10 K3, p1, LTT, p5, k1, p7, k3, p4, k7, p4, k3, p7, k1, p5, RTT, p1, k3.

Row 12 K3, p15, k3, p5, k7, p5, k3, p15, k3.

Row 14 K3, p15, k3, p6, k7, p6, k3, p15, k3.

Row 16 K3, p15, k3, p7, k7, p7, k3, p15, k3.

Row 18 K3, p7, k1, p5, RTT, p1, k3, p8, k7, p8, k3, p1, LTT, p5, k1, p7, k3.

Row 20 K3, p15, k3, p9, k7, p9, k3, p15, k3.

Row 22 K3, p15, k3, p10, k7, p10, k3, p15, k3.

Row 24 K3, p15, k3, p11, k7, p11, k3, p15, k3.

Row 26 K3, p1, LTT, p5, k1, p7, k3, p7, k1, p4, k7, p4, k1, p7, k3, p7, k1, p5, RTT, p1, k3.

Row 28 K3, p15, k3, p13, k7, p13, k3, p15, k3.

Row 30 K3, p15, k3, p14, k7, p14, k3, p15, k3.

Row 32 K3, p15, k3, p15, k7, p15, k3, p15, k3.

Row 34 K3, p7, k1, p5, RTT, p1, k3, p1, LTT, p5, k1, p7, k9, p7, k1, p5, RTT, p1, k3, p1, LTT, p5, k1, p7, k3.

Row 36 K3, p15, k3, p15, k11, p15, k3, p15, k3.

Row 38 K3, p15, k3, p15, k13, p15, k3, p15, k3.

Row 40 K3, p15, k3, p15, k3, p1, k7, p1, k3, p15, k3, p15, k3.

Row 42 K3, p1, LTT, p5, k1, p7, k3, p7, k1, p5, RTT, p1, k3, p2, k7, p2, k3, p1, LTT, p5, k1, p7, k3, p7, k1, p5, RTT, p1, k3.

Row 44 K3, p15, k3, p15, k3, p3, k7, p3, k3, p15, k3, p15, k3.

Row 46 K3, p15, k3, p15, k3, p4, k7, p4, k3, p15, k3, p15, k3.

Row 48 K3, p15, k3, p15, k3, p5, k7, p5, k3, p15, k3, p15, k3.

Row 50 K3, p7, k1, p5, RTT, p1, k3, p1, LTT, p5, k1, p7, k3, p6, k7, p6, k3, p7, k1, p5, RTT, p1, k3, p1, LTT, p5, k1, p7, k3.

Row 52 K3, p15, k3, p15, k3, p7, k7, p7, k3, p15, k3, p15, k3.

Row 54 K3, p15, k3, p15, k3, p8, k7, p8, k3, p15, k3, p15, k3.

BACK

With 2 strands of yarn held tog, cast on 43 sts.

Row 1 (RS) Knit.

Row 2 Knit.

Row 3 K20, kfb, pm, k1, kfb, k20—45 sts.

Row 4 Knit.

Row 5 K to 1 st before marker, kfb, sm, k1, kfb, k to end—47 sts.

Row 6 Knit.

Begin Basic Braid Pattern

Note 3 sts each side are worked in garter st (k every row) throughout.

Row 1 and all RS rows K to 1 st before marker, kfb, sm, k1, kfb, k to end—2 sts inc'd.

Row 2 K3, p7, k1, p7, k13, p7, k1, p7, k3.

Row 4 K3, p15, k3, p1, k7, p1, k3, p15, k3.

Row 56 K3, p15, k3, p15, k3, p9, k7, p9, k3, p15, k3, p15, k3.

Row 58 K3, p1, LTT, p5, k1, p7, k3, p7, k1, p5, RTT, p1, k3, p7, k1, p2, k7, p2, k1, p7, k3, p1, LTT, p5, k1, p7, k3, p7, k1, p5, RTT, p1, k3.

Row 60 K3, p15, k3, p15, k3, p11, k7, p11, k3, p15, k3, p15, k3.

Row 62 K3, p15, k3, p15, k3, p12, k7, p12, k3, p15, k3, p15, k3.

Row 64 K3, p15, k3, p15, k3, p13, k7, p13, k3, p15, k3, p15, k3.

Row 66 K3, p7, k1, p5, RTT, p1, k3, p1, LTT, p5, k1, p7, k3, p1, LTT, p5, k1, p6, k7, p6, k1, p5, RTT, p1, k3, p7, k1, p5, RTT, p1, k3, p1, LTT, p5, k1, p7, k3.

Row 68 K3, p15, k3, p15, k3, p15, k7, p15, k3, p15, k3, p15, k3.

Row 70 K3, p15, k3, p15, k3, p15, k9, p15, k3, p15, k3, p15, k3.

Row 72 K3, p15, k3, p15, k3, p15, k11, p15, k3, p15, k3, p15, k3.

Row 74 K3, p1, LTT, p29, RTT, p17, RTT, p1, k13, p1, LTT, p17, LLT, p29, RTT, p1, k3—121 sts.

Lower Edge

Rows 1, 3, and 5 (RS) K to 1 st before marker, kfb, sm, k1, kfb, k to end—2 sts inc'd.

Rows 2 and 4 Knit.

Bind off on foll WS row, inc before *and* after center st.

FRONTS

Note Basic braid pat for fronts can be worked from written instructions or chart.

With RS facing, pick up and k 75 sts evenly along side edge of back (pick-up row is row 1 of basic braid pat). Cont in basic braid pat as foll:

Row 2 (WS) [K3, p7, k1, p7] 4 times, k3.

Row 3 and all RS rows Knit.

Rows 4, 6, and 8 [K3, p15] 4 times, k3.

Row 10 [K3, p1, LTT, p5, k1, p7] 4 times, k3.

Rows 12, 14, and 16 [K3, p15] 4 times, k3.

Row 18 [K3, p7, k1, p5, RTT, p1] 4 times, k3.

Rows 20, 22, and 24 [K3, p15] 4 times, k3.

Row 26 [K3, p1, LTT, p5, k1, p7] 4 times, k3.

Rep rows 11–26 four times more, omitting Tuck Stitches on final row 26.

Knit 5 rows for front edging. Bind off on WS row.

Rep for 2nd front.

FINISHING

Weave in ends. Block to measurements. ◆

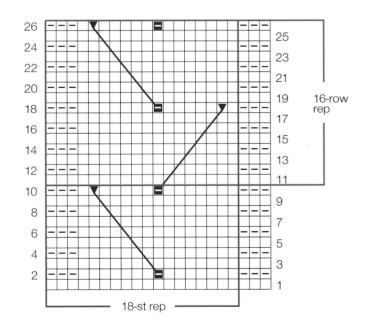

Stitch Key

☐ k on RS, p on WS

⊟ k on WS

◥ LTT on WS

◢ RTT on WS

ABBREVIATIONS & TECHNIQUES

ABBREVIATIONS

2nd	second
3rd	third
approx	approximately
beg	begin(ning)
ch	chain
cm	centimeter(s)
cont	continu(e)(ing)
dec	decreas(e)(ing)
dpn	double-pointed needle(s)
foll	follow(s)(ing)
g	gram(s)
inc	increas(e)(ing)
k	knit
k2tog	knit 2 stitches together
kfb	knit into the front and back of a stitch
LH	left-hand
lp(s)	loop(s)
m	meter(s)
M1	make 1 (knit stitch)
M1 p-st	make 1 purl stitch
mm	millimeter(s)
oz	ounce(s)
p	purl
p2tog	purl 2 stitches together
pat(s)	pattern(s)
pfb	purl into the front and back of a stitch
pm	place marker
rem	remain(s)(ing)
rep	repeat
RH	right-hand
rnd(s)	round(s)
RS	right side(s)
SK2P	slip 1, knit 2 together, pass slip stitch over the knit 2 together
sl	slip
sm	slip marker
ssk	slip the next 2 stitches one at a time knitwise to right-hand needle, knit these 2 stitches together with left-hand needle
sssk	slip the next 3 stitches one at a time knitwise to right-hand needle, knit these 3 stitches together with left-hand needle
st(s)	stitch(es)
St st	stockinette stitch
tbl	through back loop(s)
tog	together
WS	wrong side(s)
wyib	with yarn in back
wyif	with yarn in front
yd	yard(s)
yo	yarn over needle
*	repeat directions following * as many times as indicated
[ ]	repeat directions inside brackets as many times as indicated

PROVISIONAL CAST-ON

With scrap yarn and crochet hook, chain the number of stitches to cast on, plus a few extra. Cut a tail and pull the tail through the last chain stitch. With knitting needle and yarn, pick up and knit the stated number of stitches through the "purl bumps" on the back of the chain. To remove scrap chain, when instructed, pull out the tail from the last crochet stitch. Gently and slowly pull on the tail to unravel the crochet stitches, carefully placing each released knit stitch on a needle.

LONG-TAIL CAST-ON

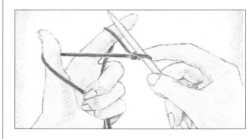

1) Make a slipknot on the right-hand needle, leaving a long tail. Wrap the tail end around your left thumb, front to back. Wrap the yarn from the ball over your left index finger. Secure both yarn ends in your palm.
2) Insert the needle upwards in the loop on your thumb. Then with the needle, draw the yarn from the ball through the loop to form a stitch.
3) Take your thumb out of the loop and tighten the loop on the needle to create a stitch. Repeat steps 2 and 3 until desired number of stitches are cast on.

KITCHENER STITCH

Cut a tail at least 4 times the length of the edge that will be grafted together and thread through a tapestry needle. Hold needles together with right sides showing, making sure each has the same number of live stitches, and work as follows:

1) Insert tapestry needle purlwise through first stitch on front needle. Pull yarn through, leaving stitch on needle.

2) Insert tapestry needle knitwise through first stitch on back needle. Pull yarn through, leaving stitch on needle.

3) Insert tapestry needle knitwise through first stitch on front needle, pull yarn through, and slip stitch off needle. Then, insert tapestry needle purlwise through next stitch on front needle and pull yarn through, leaving this stitch on needle.

4) Insert tapestry needle purlwise through first stitch on back needle, pull yarn through, and slip stitch off needle. Then, insert tapestry needle knitwise through next stitch on back needle and pull yarn through, leaving this stitch on needle.

Repeat steps 3 and 4 until all stitches on both front and back needles have been grafted.

THINGS TO KNOW

RESOURCES

Cascade Yarns
www.cascadeyarns.com

Debbie Bliss
www.debbieblissonline.com

Blue Sky Fibers
www.blueskyfibers.com

HiKoo/Skacel
www.skacelknitting.com

Jade Sapphire
www.jadesapphire.com

Noro/KFI
www.knittingfever.com/brand/noro

Rowan
www.knitrowan.com

KNITTING NEEDLES

US	Metric	US	Metric
0	2mm	9	5.5mm
1	2.25mm	10	6mm
2	2.75mm	10½	6.5mm
3	3.25mm	11	8mm
4	3.5mm	13	9mm
5	3.75mm	15	10mm
6	4mm	17	12.75mm
7	4.5mm	19	15mm
8	5mm	35	19mm

SKILL LEVELS

■□□□
BEGINNER
Ideal first project.

■■□□
EASY
Basic stitches, minimal shaping, and simple finishing.

■■■□
INTERMEDIATE
For knitters with some experience. More intricate stitches, shaping, and finishing.

■■■■
EXPERIENCED
For knitters able to work patterns with complicated shaping and finishing.

STANDARDS & GUIDELINES FOR CROCHET AND KNITTING

STANDARD YARN WEIGHT SYSTEM

Yarn Weight Symbol & Category	0 Lace	1 Super Fine	2 Fine	3 Light	4 Medium	5 Bulky	6 Super Bulky	7 Jumbo
Type of Yarns in Category	Fingering 10-count crochet thread	Sock, Fingering, Baby	Sport, Baby	DK, Light Worsted	Worsted, Afghan, Aran	Chunky, Craft, Rug	Super Bulky, Roving	Jumbo, Roving
Knit Gauge Range* in Stockinette Stitch to 4 inches	33–40** sts	27–32 sts	23–26 sts	21–24 sts	16–20 sts	12–15 sts	7–11 sts	6 sts and fewer
Recommended Needle in Metric Size Range	1.5–2.25 mm	2.25—3.25 mm	3.25—3.75 mm	3.75—4.5 mm	4.5—5.5 mm	5.5—8 mm	8—12.75 mm	12.75 mm and larger
Recommended Needle U.S. Size Range	000–1	1 to 3	3 to 5	5 to 7	7 to 9	9 to 11	11 to 17	17 and larger
Crochet Gauge* Ranges in Single Crochet to 4 inch	32–42 double crochets**	21–32 sts	16–20 sts	12–17 sts	11–14 sts	8–11 sts	6–9 sts	5 sts and fewer
Recommended Hook in Metric Size Range	Steel*** 1.6–1.4 mm	2.25—3.5 mm	3.5—4.5 mm	4.5—5.5 mm	5.5—6.5 mm	6.5—9 mm	9—16 mm	16 mm and larger
Recommended Hook U.S. Size Range	Steel*** 6, 7, 8 Regular hook B–1	B–1 to E–4	E–4 to 7	7 to I–9	I–9 to K–10 1/2	K–10 1/2 to M–13	M–13 to Q	Q and larger

* GUIDELINES ONLY: The above reflect the most commonly used gauges and needle or hook sizes for specific yarn categories.

** Lace weight yarns are usually knitted or crocheted on larger needles and hooks to create lacy, openwork patterns. Accordingly, a gauge range is difficult to determine. Always follow the gauge stated in your pattern.

*** Steel crochet hooks are sized differently from regular hooks—the higher the number, the smaller the hook, which is the reverse of regular hook sizing

This Standards & Guidelines booklet and downloadable symbol artwork are available at: **YarnStandards.com**

CHECKING YOUR GAUGE

Make a test swatch at least 4"/10cm square. If the number of stitches and rows does not correspond to gauge given, you must change the needle size. An easy rule to follow is: To get fewer stitches to the inch/cm, use a larger needle; to get more stitches to the inch/cm, use a smaller needle. Continue to try different needle sizes until you get the same number of stitches and rows in the gauge. See page 15 for more information on checking gauge over Dimensional Tuck stitch patterns.

INDEX

ACKNOWLEDGEMENTS

Developing something like Dimensional Tuck Knitting is a long, singularly focused process requiring an enormous amount of help and support from many, many people.

My heartfelt thanks go out to Dana Baldwin for the boundless support, enthusiasm, and encouragement she gave so freely and frequently. Being able to give me knitterly advice and being ready to edit anything I gave her at a moment's notice was a godsend. You were there on day one. I owe you big time, Woman. Much love.

When it came time to approach a publisher, it was Laura Bryant who gave me the courage to do so, and who freely shared her knowledge and experience. Having you believe in me has kept me going since the first day we met, and you have my thanks for all eternity.

Without Trisha Malcolm, Dimensional Tuck Knitting would just be a lot of swatches in a box in my house. Trisha listened to my 30-second elevator spiel and immediately started the ball rolling, going against the norm and taking a chance on a first-time author. I am forever grateful and hope I have exceeded your expectations.

Jacob Seifert, I think I love you. Having an editor is a scary thing, but you put me at ease and made everything fun. Thank you!

Carla Scott, you have done a phenomenal job understanding my vision and translating my rough-hewn charts into something wonderful. Wow!

The staff at Soho Publishing and Sixth&Spring are the best, going above and beyond to pull this rough manuscript into shape. I am forever grateful for your expertise.

A universe of thanks to my family, all of you, for your constant love and encouragement, even though I was a little distracted at times.

But mostly I am thankful for Joe, who loves me without fail, indulges me without thought, and tries really hard to understand knitting.

AUTHOR BIO

*"My goal as a designer is
to make people think, or at the very least,
to consider the possibilities."*

Tracy Purtscher has been creating garments her entire
life, beginning when her father taught her to sew at a very
young age. By the age of seven, she was mending clothing
for the members of her large family of seven children; a
few years later she was making most of her own clothes.
In high school, Tracy taught herself how to crochet with a
paper clip and a piece of string while in detention. Knitting,
however, eluded her for many years until she discovered
a vintage magazine with a how-to section for continental
knitting that finally made things click.

Since she took up knitting needles, Tracy Purtscher has
been designing stunning garments. Her designs have
appeared in numerous publications, including *knit.purl*,
Simply Knitting, *Noro*, and *Vogue Knitting*. In 2013, she
was a finalist on the *Fiber Factor*, a *Project Runway*-esque
knitwear-design reality web series. In 2015, she won a
Chanel-inspired design contest in *Vogue Knitting* magazine
for Burke, a chic pullover with an allover mosaic pattern
and unique zipper detail. Tracy also runs the knitting blog
Stringativity, which features her designs and musings on
knitting and creativity.